"Let's face it, widows are easy to overlo
tunately, that is increasingly true due to
the West. But the Bible is clear—taking c
biblical imperative. Croft and Walker ha
biblical foundation for caring for widows and
and practical guidelines on how to do that in your church. This is an important book for all pastors and lay leaders or any believer committed to reaching out to widows in their church and community."

Bob Russell, Former Senior Pastor, Southeast Christian Church, Louisville, Kentucky

"This book is a wonderful, in-depth guide explaining an important aspect of what Scripture calls 'true religion,' that is, to visit and care for widows in their distress. Both theological and practical, this is one of the best resources on the topic and is a must read for churches not only seeking to be compassionate, but to faithfully practice biblical justice."

Nathan Ivey, Pastor of Mercy, Sojourn Community Church

"Every Sunday as I look at my congregation, I am keenly aware of the women (and men) who have lost their beloved spouses in recent years. They are lonely. They are mourning still. They may even feel awkward among God's family. I am so thankful for this book, which reminds pastors and churches that we have a biblical mandate to love these dear ones, ministering the Word, by the Spirit, so that widows are cared for temporally in light of eternity."

Jay S. Thomas, Lead Pastor, Chapel Hill Bible Church, Chapel Hill, North Carolina

"This is a gem of a book, full of helpful advice when it comes to pastoring, loving, and caring for widows in our congregations. I personally found it challenging, and I can see it being a helpful tool in teaching church members about their responsibilities to the widows in our midst."

Mez McConnell, Senior Pastor, Niddrie Community Church, Edinburgh, Scotland; Founder, 20schemes

"While reading this book, I went 'Ouch!' more than once because it points out ways in which we have been negligent in looking after the widows in our church. This is certainly one area in which we need reformation. I trust that my 'Ouch!' will be turned into action so that God may smile at our church as he sees the way we will begin to look after widows in distress in our midst. All of us who are church elders and deacons need to get back to this religion that is pure and undefiled before God!"

Conrad Mbewe, Senior Pastor, Kabwata Baptist Church in Zambia, Africa

"We see them in the congregation; they rarely sit together; they occupy their customary place; and they have many friends. They are examples in femininity, humility, usefulness, and faith in a heavenly Father. They are the widows, but shudder at being labeled as such. They look to their preachers for the gospel message to exalt Jesus Christ. They look to their pastors for total respect and graciousness. They look to their fellow members for holy love and genuine friendship. They look to be remembered within the nuances of the body of Christ. This is what Croft and Walker enable us to do, to become better pilgrims on our way to the blessed gathering of all the elect, to be unashamed at the great reunion. 'Well done for helping widows in their affliction.' We need such help in this area, and then we find that increased thoughtfulness in one dimension encourages consecrated words and feelings in very different relationships within the holy body."

Geoff Thomas, Pastor, Alfred Place Baptist Church, Wales

CARING FOR WIDOWS

CARING FOR WIDOWS

MINISTERING GOD'S GRACE

BRIAN CROFT AND
AUSTIN WALKER

FOREWORD BY MIKE MCKINLEY

Evangelical Press

First published by Crossway in 2015

This edition published in Great Britain in 2023

British Cataloguing in Publication Data
A record for this book is available from the British Library

ISBN: 978-1-78397-423-8

Cover designed by Jude May

Printed in the UK

Evangelical Press, an imprint of 10Publishing
Unit C, Tomlinson Road, Leyland, PR25 2DY, England
epbooks@10ofthose.com
www.epbooks.org

1 3 5 7 10 8 6 4 2

Contents

Part 2

Pastoral Application—Brian Croft

Foreword

A year ago, I did not think I needed this book. Our church was mostly comprised of young, healthy people; the few elderly women in our midst were active and low maintenance. But when our congregation merged with another local church whose most prominent members were widows, I realized how much I did not know about caring for these elderly saints. There is probably no group in the church that I naturally relate to less than widows. After all, I have been young, I have been single, I have been married, and I have had children. But I've never been a woman, I've never been elderly and in poor health, and I've never lost a spouse. I know that the Lord calls me as a pastor to lead our church to care for the widows in our midst, but what could I possibly know about caring for people whose daily experience is so very different from my own? For this reason, I am very grateful that Austin Walker and Brian Croft have written this book. They have both faithfully practiced what they preach when it comes to caring for widows, and their experience shines through on every page.

The first part, a careful and clear presentation of the biblical mandate for widow care, landed like a punch between my eyes. It convicted me that I am guilty of an ungodly tendency toward indifference to the needs of these elderly saints. It's not that I don't care, but as a pastor I am often preoccupied with a crowded schedule of appointments and study obligations. I don't often go looking for people who might be suffering quietly. I don't often think about ways our church could creatively care for the widows in our midst. But if our God declares himself to be the protector of the widow and if he was indignant when Israel failed to care for its widows, then how can his church claim to represent him if we do not care for the widows in our midst? I was left with the clear impression that I need to do so.

If the first part of the book was helpfully disquieting, the second half of the book laid out an encouraging path forward to change. Written with a voice of wisdom and pastoral sensitivity, it answers almost every practical question you could have. Do you want advice on the differences you'll experience visiting widows in nursing homes as opposed to the hospital? You'll find practical advice in these pages. Do you want a suggestion about what to write in a note you leave at the hospital if you arrive and the widow you are visiting is unavailable? You'll find it in these pages. Like every volume in the Practical Shepherding ministry, this book is a veritable field guide to faithful pastoring.

The widows in my congregation owe a debt of gratitude to the authors of this book. They will doubtless receive better care as a result of their pastor reading it.

So if you are involved in church leadership in any capacity, you should stop reading this foreword and start reading the book itself. The widows in your church will thank you!

Mike McKinley
Sterling Park Baptist Church
Sterling, Virginia

Introduction

There are many exciting and encouraging evidences of late that Jesus Christ is at work through his Spirit in his church. There is a recovery of biblical preaching. Churches are making membership more meaningful, which has led to the recovery of church discipline in many congregations. The gospel is being more clearly preached, and this has led not just to conversions but intentional discipleship of those new converts in local churches. No one can deny the explosion of fruitful mercy ministries in many churches that has led to a more proactive effort to care for the poor, adopt orphans, and seek to remedy the homeless, hurting, and oppressed. Truly the Lord continues to build his church, and these are but a few of the many signs of this unstoppable work.

There are, however, chinks in the armor of these encouraging recoveries. The recovery of biblical preaching in some churches is the result of a pragmatic approach to the church that might fade when the next fad arrives. Faithful gospel preaching in some circles appears to be a reaction to the crushing effects of legalism in the church and quite possibly represents a swing that might squeeze out any rigorous pursuit of holiness in the next generation. This fresh emergence of intentional mercy ministry in the church has led, on the one hand, to a greater extent of care by God's people to orphans, the poor, and the oppressed. On the other hand, widows do not always receive the care that God expects his people to provide.

For some reason, a large portion of the evangelical church has missed the biblical warrant to care for widows, while still engaging in care for the fatherless and the poor. Even those who see widows as being among those whom God particularly calls his people to protect, provide for, and nurture still sometimes fail to make it a priority. In part, this neglect could stem from an inability to know how best to care for a widow. As a result, widows still remain largely overlooked and forgotten in the church. The aim of this book is to accomplish two goals: (1) to inform the reader of the biblical imperatives upon God's people for this task, and then (2) give practical helps on how pastors and church leaders can particularly minister to widows. But before going any further, an answer to the most obvious question about this issue is necessary—who is a widow?

Compassion in a Fallen World

A widow is a married woman whose husband has died and who remains unmarried. In the Bible, mourning, weeping, and a sense of desolation, disillusionment, bitterness, loneliness, and helplessness were often experienced by a widow following the death of her spouse. The loss of a husband was often a social and economic tragedy. Once the main source of her financial support was lost, the widow often fell into debt and poverty. Becoming a widow made her vulnerable. In the Bible, she was frequently placed alongside similar people in need such as the stranger (the landless immigrant) and the fatherless (e.g., Ex. 22:21–22; Deut. 24:17–21). Her plight could be aggravated further if she had no able-bodied children to help her work the land of her former husband. Because of all these changed circumstances, widows were often marginalized. Therefore, it is not surprising to find that in ancient Israel they were regarded as being in need of special protection.

We live in a fallen world where, sadly, death destroys earthly friendships and relationships. Few circumstances in life are more devastating than the death of a husband. Of course, a husband also experiences grief and feels acutely that sense of desolation arising from the loss of his best friend and closest companion—his wife. Thus we find, for example, that Abraham mourned and wept for his Sarah (Gen. 23:2). The Bible has comparatively little to say about living as a widower, however, and much more to say about being a widow. One reason for this distinction is the fact that a widower is not in the same vulnerable position as a widow.

When the Lord God first made this world, he made Adam and then formed Eve from the body of Adam. They became husband and wife, and as long as they continued in obedience to God, death did not threaten to separate them. Once they had sinned against God, however, death entered the created world. Adam was to live for 930 years (Gen. 5:5). Was Eve widowed? The Scriptures remain silent. Since the fall, however, widowhood has become a permanent reality in this world.

The Hebrew word translated "widow" is *almana*, and it occurs over fifty times in the Old Testament. The Greek word for widow is *chera*, which is used twenty-six times in the New Testament. It is vocabulary that belongs to this fallen world. In biblical times the terms for "widow" sometimes acquired the connotation of a person living in extreme poverty. While this was not always the case, widows were nevertheless prime targets for exploitation. It was because of this vulnerable state that God himself took steps to secure the protection of widows, commanding his people to show compassion and sensitivity toward them in their need.

Are widows as vulnerable today as they were in former days? Does the twenty-first-century church have any particular responsibilities toward widows, or does the passing of time and the inevitable changes in culture mean that such considerations are no longer relevant? The lot of widows in the Western world may have improved in many ways, but ongoing needs remain despite those improvements. Meanwhile, the plight of widows in other parts of the world continues with widows invariably exposed to suffering from neglect, abuse, and various forms of exploitation.

Every widow experiences grief and invariably feels overwhelmed by sorrow. The transition from being a wife to living as a widow (even if remarriage eventually takes place) is fraught with all kinds of problems. To come to terms with the new situation takes time and is often the occasion when widows most need a patient, listening ear, together with sympathy and wise, sensitive counsel. For example, many widows cry out, "Why me?" and, feeling intense anger and frustration, are ready to accuse God of unkindness. Others suddenly find themselves overwhelmed and swamped with decisions about everyday matters to do with the house or the car, which their husbands usually handled. Still others face the responsibilities of handling the finances with fear and trepidation, and sadly, some have to face the horror of discovering that their spouse did not leave the finances in good order.

Whether the church should cultivate a distinctive ministry to widows is not only to be determined by the sad experiences and trials of widows following the death of their husbands, but also by what God says in his Word. God is described as "a father of the fatherless, a defender of widows" (Ps. 68:5). That one verse alone alerts us to the fact that, as far as God is concerned, widows are the special object of his protection and care. It would seem reasonable to conclude therefore, that if widows are the concern of God in his holy habitation, then it would be a major failing on the part of the church of Christ—not only her elders, but also her deacons, together with every member of the body of Christ—if they shrugged their shoulders and went on quietly with their own lives, ignoring the needs of widows.

The widow, the orphan, and the poor were covered by laws that protected them in other ancient Near Eastern cultures such as Sumer in Mesopotamia and later in the law code of Hammurabi in the eighteenth century BC. In Egypt, their protection was often the boast of the beneficent king. For example, Rameses III claimed that he had given special attention to securing justice for them.[1] When we look at the biblical texts dealing with the widow, the orphan, and the poor, however, God introduced another element. His concerns for them are embedded in sections of Scripture that deal with the covenant made between God, the sovereign Lord, and his people, Israel, both in the covenant law given at Sinai and at the renewal of the covenant before entering into the land of Canaan.

Religious and social ethics were closely bound together in the ancient world even among the pagan nations. Israel was unique as a nation, and we need to recognize that her social ethic stemmed directly from the Lord of the covenant, her Redeemer. In today's world the danger for the church is that she responds to the needs of the widow only on the basis of broad humanitarian aid. In the secularization of the Western world, religion has become divorced from social concerns and conduct. The Scriptures take us beyond mere humanitarian help, as we shall see in subsequent chapters.

Therefore, the purpose of chapters 1–10 (part 1) is to explore the duties of the church toward widows and provide a biblical mandate for churches to develop a specific ministry for widows, especially those within the household of faith. Furthermore, if widows are not to be deprived of the comfort that comes from knowing that their God is the God who really cares for them, then this part will also form the substance of what must be taught to them. The rest of the book, chapters 11–20 (part 2), provides hands-on counsel and practical advice on how to develop a ministry to widows in your congregation. Although this book is written with a ministry to widows specifically in mind, you will find much of what is written here can contribute in other ministries to hurting people. Additionally, these biblical and practical principles can be applied to the care of widowers (men whose wives have died) as well.

Furthermore, the authors are aware that the plight of a widow in many other nations, for example in the African continent and Indian subcontinent, is often far more distressing and severe than in the West. We have not attempted to address these situations in part 2. However, we would underline that the biblical principles outlined in part 1 are universal in their application.

Finally, our prayer is that this slim volume will lead to a more fruitful effort to minister God's grace to all the hurting and neglected people to whom God reveals his tender love and divine care through his redeemed people for his glory.

Part 1

The Biblical Warrant

Austin Walker

1

Christ's Example and James's Principle

The Lord Jesus Christ serves as the model and example for his church. He took particular note of widows. We may think of the widow in the temple with her two mites (Mark 12:41–44); the widow of Nain, whose one remaining son was restored to life (Luke 17:11–17); and the widow in the parable about persistent prayer (Luke 18:1–8). Sometimes widows were on the receiving end of injustice. It is no surprise, therefore, to hear how Christ exposed the scribes and Pharisees because some of them were exploiting widows (Mark 12:40). Additionally, the words he spoke and the actions he took regarding his own mother while he hung dying on the cross demonstrate to us how like his heavenly Father Jesus really was. He was full of understanding and compassion and, as a faithful son, acted to ensure Mary's needs were met.

This moving episode is recorded in the latter part of John's Gospel (19:26–27). Despite all of Christ's sufferings and agonies, he remained selfless and occupied himself with the needs of different people. For example, he considered Peter and the disciples who had all scattered like frightened sheep. There was the penitent thief alongside him. In particular, Jesus entered into the sorrows of his mother as he hung on the cross. At this point in her life, she was almost certainly widowed. Why did Jesus give a sacred charge to John to treat Mary as his own mother? It was because there was no husband or other family in a position to care and to provide for her after his death. The Lord Jesus was fulfilling his obligations to his mother with demonstrable filial love and great tenderness of heart, obeying the fifth commandment in the process. John's response was immediate. We read that "from that hour that disciple took her to his own home" (v. 27).

The Lord Jesus did not choose to provide Mary with silver, gold, or any other precious possessions that might have been a means of supporting her now that she was alone. Rather, he ensured she was cared for in a secure home by the man who was recognized as being the disciple closest to Jesus and was perhaps the most loving and tenderhearted of those men.

Here in the Lord Jesus Christ is the priceless example of care for widows that, as we shall see, reflects everything the Scriptures teach in both the Old and the New Testaments. Can the church of Christ turn a blind eye to such an example?

Compassion for Widows: A Vital Principle of True Religion

The pattern for the church's conduct is also established by the principle laid down by James: "Pure and undefiled religion before God and the Father is this: to visit orphans and widows in their trouble, and to keep oneself unspotted from the world" (1:27). James explains the nature of religion that God accepts as genuine. It is interesting that he does not give us a full picture but instead focuses on two aspects of true piety that demonstrate what it means to "be doers of the word" (1:22). "To visit orphans and widows" is one vital part of that true religion.

This involves far more, however, than dropping in on an occasional friendly social call. The term "visit" in the Greek was used to describe the action of a doctor who, in visiting sick patients, showed care for them and supplied their needs. James intends his readers to understand that these visits should be deliberate, involving regular personal contact and practical involvement with those in need. This principle was given to ensure that appropriate sympathy and relief was ministered to widows and orphans.

The reason for this care is given in the same breath—orphans and widows face trouble that is peculiar to their situation. Such visits were intended, then, to alleviate their distress—in this case, their difficult, trying circumstances; their grief; and their loneliness. In addition, it meant taking steps to ensure that they did not become the victims of unscrupulous individuals (even family members, in some cases) who would take advantage of their situations and exploit them. As will become more evident in this book, orphans and widows represented two of the most needy groups in the ancient world. The Old Testament Scriptures provide the backdrop and examples to the situations that James only touches on here.

If God himself is the defender of widows (Ps. 68:5) and shows compassion for them as discussed in the introduction, then the church of the Lord Jesus Christ can scarcely turn its back on their troubles. Rather, Christians should reflect their heavenly Father and their Redeemer, Jesus Christ. Such compassion and love ought to be freely, cheerfully, and willingly displayed and know not to expect to be repaid. "Widows who are really widows" (1 Tim. 5:3), according to the Bible's definition, are almost invariably not in any position to return material favors.

2

The Price for Neglecting Widows

One of the oldest books in the Old Testament is the book of Job. There we find that Job was accused of wickedness by Eliphaz. By neglecting to relieve widows (22:9) together with other sins, Eliphaz claimed that Job had brought God's judgment down on his own head. Job vigorously denied Eliphaz's explanation for his sufferings, and later on, referring to his alleged treatment of widows, called on God to visit him in judgment if indeed he was guilty of such wickedness (e.g., Job 31:16).

Job was innocent. Although Eliphaz wrongly accused Job, he was right in principle. There *is* a price to be paid for neglecting and abusing widows. If God is the defender of widows, he will not turn a blind eye or deaf ear to their cries.

God's Indignation at the Ill-Treatment of Widows

On several occasions the Old Testament prophets exposed Israel's wickedness because of the ways in which Israel had treated the widow, the orphan, and the poor.[2] Anyone who ignored the cause of the widow, who oppressed her, who preyed on and exploited her, or who ill-treated her in any manner was flying directly in the face of God and could expect to be confronted with his curse and judgment.

There was a price to be paid for such ill-treatment. Isaiah, Jeremiah, and Ezekiel spoke of the judgment of God that came with the exile. While the ways the widow was treated was not the sole cause of the exile, it was one of the sins highlighted by the Holy One of Israel. The people's failure to uphold the cause of the widow was placed alongside other sins such as shedding innocent blood, following after other gods, practicing immorality, profaning God's Sabbaths, and indulging in bribery. For these and all their sins, Israel was scattered among the nations.

Jeremiah actually warns his contemporaries on the eve of the exile that because they have forsaken God, they will be destroyed, winnowed like grain with a fan, and their widows will be increased (Jer. 15:7–9). It is a telling and sorrowful exclamation in the opening words of Jeremiah's lament over ruined Jerusalem: "How lonely sits the city that was full of people! How like a widow is she, who was great among the nations!" (Lam. 1:1).

God's Warnings Given by Moses

What happened in the days of the prophets was not an unexpected bolt from the blue. The prophets were only bringing to bear God's words spoken much earlier through Moses.[3] The Lord God entered into covenant with his people and gave them his laws and commandments. Grafted into the laws were clear instructions about the treatment of the poor—including the stranger, the fatherless, and the widow. Anyone who perverted the justice due to any in these vulnerable groups would find a divine curse resting on him. The Lord was jealous in defending the widow and intolerant of any ill-treatment of her. He reminded the people that they had been loved by him when they were strangers in the land of Egypt and that they were to reflect the same love in their care for the stranger, the fatherless, and the widow in their midst.

The plainest language was used in Exodus 22:21–24:

> You shall neither mistreat a stranger nor oppress him, for you were strangers in the land of Egypt. You shall not afflict any widow or fatherless child. If you afflict them in any way, and they cry at all to Me, I will surely hear their cry; and My wrath will become hot, and I will kill you with the sword; your wives shall be widows, and your children fatherless.

Such a warning explains what happened to Israel in the days of the prophets. The Lord declared that not only will he hear their cry and come to their defense, but he will take vengeance on those who are responsible. Tragically, that is exactly what happened in the captivity and exile of the nation of Israel. Many of the men were killed and their wives and children left desolate as widows and orphans. There was and is a price to be paid by those who neglect or ill-treat those whom God defends.

The Implications for the Church Today

Passages like these, together with the positive commands regarding widows (which we shall consider later in chapter 5), composed the Old Testament teachings that formed the attitude of the dying Savior toward his mother and also of James as he set out the practice of genuine religion in his epistle (1:27). In light of the warnings given by Moses and the prophets, it would be unthinkable for the incarnate Son of God to neglect the care of his widowed mother. James was aware that there is a form of religion that is useless. He would not have hesitated, therefore, to identify with Jeremiah and the other prophets in exposing the hollowness of their contemporaries.

Given these warnings from Moses and the prophets, together with the example of the Lord Jesus Christ and the rule laid down by James, the church of Christ cannot evade the implications which inevitably follow. For elders, deacons, and church members to neglect or ill-treat widows expresses an attitude that is not only the total opposite of the conduct of God the Father and of the Lord Jesus Christ, but it invites the chastening hand of God and calls into question the integrity of the church and her identity as the people of God. The neglect of widows is not specifically mentioned by the risen, reigning Son of Man as something he has against any of the seven churches of Asia in Revelation 2 and 3. However, given the similarity of some of the other sins he holds against the seven churches with the sins mentioned in the Prophets, would it be too much to say that the neglect of widows could provide a reason for him to remove our lampstand from its place? Is there not a price to be paid if we give no heed to what he says about the care of widows?

3

The Compassion of Boaz

The compassion of God toward widows was not only displayed by the ways in which he surrounds them with protection in his Word, threatening punishment to those who continually disregard his commandments and who continue to take advantage of vulnerable widows. There are also some marvelous examples in the Scriptures of the way he uses good men to help those who are in need because death intruded into their daily lives. Boaz, Elijah, and Elisha were three such men. Remarkably, two of the women concerned are widows from outside the borders of Israel: one is Ruth the Moabitess and the other the widow of Zarephath, which belonged to Sidon. Elisha ministered to a widow of one of the sons of the prophets. In this chapter, we will take up the story of Naomi and Ruth.

The Sorrows of Mrs. "Mara"

When Naomi returned from Moab to Bethlehem after an absence of ten years, she returned a broken and sorrowful woman. Three deaths and three funerals loomed large in her heart and memory. The story unfolds in the first chapter of Ruth. Having left Bethlehem at a time of famine, Elimelech (Naomi's husband) took refuge across the Jordan in Moab. Elimelech died in Moab, however, leaving Naomi alone with her two sons, Mahlon and Chilion. No doubt her hopes rose when her sons married Orpah and Ruth, even though they were Moabite women. At least there would be the possibility of grandsons raised up in her family. But soon her hopes were dashed to the ground and her sorrows multiplied! Both Mahlon and Chilion died, leaving her bereft of her husband and her two sons.

Having heard that the famine back home was over, she began the journey back to Bethlehem. She counseled her daughters-in-law to return to Moab, not least because "the hand of the Lord has gone out against me!" (1:13). Orpah returned, but Ruth was determined to stay with her mother-in-law. Ruth's moving pleas and her confession of Naomi's God as her God indicated that Ruth had decisively turned her back on the idols of Moab (1:16–17).

The joys of returning home and the excitement of Naomi's friends when they saw her again after so many years were tempered by the severe losses Naomi had endured. She told the women firmly,

> Do not call me Naomi; call me Mara, for the Almighty has dealt very bitterly with me. I went out full, and the Lord has brought me home again empty. Why do you call me Naomi, since the Lord has testified against me, and the Almighty has afflicted me? (1:20–21)

Naomi means "pleasant" but Mara means "bitterness," and her self-appointed name sums up how she felt and interpreted God's dealings with her and her family. There is a peculiar pathos in the words of chapter 1, verse 3. Following the death of her husband, "she was left." A sense of destitution, of isolation, and of loneliness overtook her spirit. Subsequent events had done nothing to diminish any of these. She had been shaken in the depths of her being and her grief was intense and all-pervading.

Enter Boaz, the Redeemer

When she left Bethlehem, Naomi had no idea of the tragedies that would strike her one after the other in Moab. Neither did she have any inkling of the blessings that God was about to bestow upon her and upon Ruth. Naomi did not remarry, but Ruth did. In the process, they came to learn that God was the kind of God who cared for the widow, and a Father who understood the needs and emotions of grieving women. They discovered God's compassion and found refuge under the shadow of the wings of the Lord God of Israel.

Boaz was the man who mirrored a godlike compassion to Ruth. He showed concern for Ruth and protected her from any abuse. As a redeemer, he took upon himself the care and protection of a childless widow. The laws of Moses provided for a redeemer—someone who was a responsible next of kin who was expected to fulfill various family duties. For example, a redeemer acted in order to maintain the family line and to recover property that was lost or about to be lost to the family (Lev. 25:23–34).[4]

Boaz took up the cause of Ruth and Naomi. In their case, this involved redeeming the property of Elimelech. He also undertook to marry Ruth, exercising a levirate kind of responsibility (Genesis 38; Deut. 25:5–10).[5] He had let her glean in the fields and had provided drink for her when she was thirsty and food when she was hungry. In acting in this manner, he was consciously obeying the law of Moses and the provision that Israelites were to make for widows (Deut. 24:21–22). It was Naomi who blessed the Lord when she realized that Boaz was one of their close relatives (Ruth 2:20).

Boaz was a man who clearly feared the Lord, because he obeyed God's commandments. We could say that here was "pure and undefiled religion before God and the Father" as described in James 1:27. The life of Boaz was governed by the Lord of the covenant and his Word. As a result, Boaz demonstrated true love and faithfulness, imitating his divine Redeemer. He went beyond the demands of the letter of the law because he was a highly motivated man who understood the covenant faithfulness of the Lord and the implications that it had for him as a close relative of Naomi and now Ruth—even though she was a Moabitess.

Boaz raised up children to Elimelech. The women of Bethlehem let their joy be known when Ruth conceived and bore a son, Obed. They blessed the Lord because of his provision of a close relative. The Lord had not abandoned Naomi and had even included Ruth.

In the providence of God, Ruth had come to glean in the fields of Boaz, and ultimately it was the Lord who cared for and protected Ruth as she came under his wings to find refuge (Ruth 2:12). By trusting in the Lord, even though she was a Moabite widow, she participated in forming the house of David. Obed was the grandfather of King David, from whom the Messiah, Jesus Christ, came (Ruth 4:17; cf. Matt. 1:1, 5–6).

The purpose of the book of Ruth is clearly bigger than simply demonstrating God's compassion for the widow. Nevertheless, it does display the reasons why the Lord established the levirate laws and the institution of the redeemer—the next of kin—with family responsibilities. The story of Ruth abundantly illustrates the covenant faithfulness and compassion of the Lord. Even though these exact provisions given to Israel no longer apply to us today, it does not mean that we can suspend showing compassion to widows who are in particular need.

4

The Compassion of Elijah and Elisha

First Kings 17 provides us with another striking Old Testament example of God's compassion for the widow. This particular widow's plight was acute. Famine had left Israel and the surrounding area, including Zarephath in Sidon, in a desperate condition. This solitary widow and her one son faced starvation and certain death. She probably was thin, emaciated, and quietly resigned to her inevitable lot. Two more victims of the famine would perhaps hardly be noticed.

Elijah, the prophet, had pronounced a drought on the land at God's command. It was a judgment specifically against King Ahab, who was more wicked than any of his royal predecessors (1 Kings 16:30). Up to that point, Elijah had been sustained by ravens bringing him a meal twice a day in the form of meat and bread as he remained in hiding by the brook Cherith. When the brook dried up, the Lord told him a widow in Zarephath would now provide for his needs. On finding her, the prophet interrupted her pathetic search for a few sticks of wood in order to light a fire and cook what she thought would be the last meal for herself and her son.

The Lord Jesus knew this story well. In Luke 4:25–26, he related how Elijah had not been sent to widows in Israel during the famine but to a Gentile widow in territory under the rule of the idolatrous king of Sidon. Like Ruth before her, she was to discover that the God of Israel was the living God and that he alone could deliver her and her son from death. Once again, we have before us a gripping story that makes the point that God cares for the widow and is ready to show his power and kindness when it is least expected.

The Provision Made for This Widow

When Elijah first spoke to her, he made what seemed to be an outrageous request. Finding her outside the city gate gathering sticks, he asked her to bring him some water in a cup and some bread in her hand to feed *him*. She related to him that it would be impossible for her to make such provision as she and her son had next to nothing left for themselves, let alone enough to share with a stranger. Telling her not to be afraid, Elijah instructed her to complete the task of collecting the sticks, return home, prepare the food, and then give him the first helping! Only after that would she and her son eat what she had prepared.

In the next breath, Elijah explained to her that the Lord would provide for her, her son, and also for Elijah. The bin of flour would not run out and the jar of oil would not run dry until the famine was over (1 Kings 17:14). This widow did exactly as she was instructed, and the Lord did everything he had promised. By such means the Lord provided for his servant Elijah, and the widow and her son were kept from death.

The Lord did not despise this lady because she was a widow nor because she was a Gentile. She was not well known (we do not even know her name) and she certainly was not rich, but the Lord chose to honor this poor woman and record his kindness to her in the Scriptures. She provided bed and board for Elijah for perhaps as long as two years. In this way she, like Ruth, came to know the God of Israel. She learned to trust the Lord and obey his word and continued to live by faith.

The Widow's Son Restored to Life

The miraculous supply of flour and oil could stave off hunger, but it did not prevent the eventual sickness and death of her son. Now she faced a new crisis, and it was more than she could take. She spoke hastily against Elijah. Forgetting past mercies and the miraculous daily provision, it now seemed to her as if God was playing cruel tricks and could no longer be trusted. She resorted to thinking that God was now punishing her for her sins and blamed Elijah for the death of her son.

Elijah took her son in his arms, carried him to the upper room where he was staying, and cried out to God for the life of the young man to be restored. The widow was a new woman when Elijah brought her son back down to her alive. Not only was her son restored to life, but her faith in God was also restored.

Earlier King Ahab had accused Elijah of being the "troubler of Israel," and Elijah's reply showed that he could be as bold as a lion (1 Kings 18:17–19). On that occasion he was facing extreme wickedness, but here his character was marked by tenderness of spirit as he faced the vulnerability of two needy humans, totally helpless in the face of famine and death. He recognized this widow's troubles and felt them acutely. He spoke to God as the one who had "brought tragedy on the widow with whom I lodge" (17:20). Like Boaz before him, he was well acquainted with the laws of Moses and the merciful heart of God toward widows in their distress and need. He reflected the heart of the God who sent him to the widow. Elijah knew that once the drought was over and he had left the widow, she would have been all alone. Her son was her only means of support and comfort.

By virtue of Elijah's care and concern, this widow came

to know the living God. Like Ruth she, also a Gentile, possessed a glowing testimony to the character and conduct of the God of Israel—particularly his kindness, compassion, and power.

A Widow of One of the Sons of the Prophets

Elisha was also called on to provide for and protect a widow—in this case an Israelite—a wife of one of the sons of the prophets (2 Kings 4:1–7). Plunged into poverty, she faced the prospect of losing her two sons. In order to pay her creditors, her two sons would be taken and made slaves. This passage drives home once again that God is the helper of the helpless and the nameless. Her situation was made even more difficult by the fact that her husband had been a faithful man of God at a time when such faithfulness was costly. She may have had many questions in her mind about God's dealings with her, but regardless of any doubts she cried out to Elisha, the prophet. At her wits' end, she trusted in God and his servant.

Elisha told her to go and borrow empty jars from her neighbors and then to start pouring oil into the empty jars, one after the other, filling the jars from her one remaining jar of oil, until there were no more jars left. Elisha then gave her three commands: she was to sell the oil, pay off her debts, and live on what was left over. Through this miracle, the Lord supplied not only her immediate needs but her on-going needs as well.

In the next chapter we shall discover that God made provision for widows by ordinary means as well and that Israel was to ensure that widows were not left without food. In the case of these two widows, however, their distress was so great that it was totally beyond human help. The Lord, the defender of widows, came to their rescue. These are but a few examples of his abundant, overflowing kindness to the poor and needy.

5

Provision and Protection in the Law of Moses

We have already considered the message of judgment that the prophets of Israel announced to a nation that rejected God's word and neglected or ill-treated widows. The prophets were not creating new laws but implementing existing ones that had been given to the redeemed nation by their covenant Lord in the days of Moses. Unable to announce blessings because Israel had forsaken God and refused to repent, they were bringing the curses of the covenant to bear on the sins of the nation.

Attention so far has focused on the conduct of Boaz, Elijah, and Elisha toward particular widows, showing that it was patterned after the Lord himself and also found expression in laws and procedures established by Moses. We have also seen that the Lord Jesus Christ was well acquainted with his scriptural responsibilities toward his mother and, in light of that, it was unthinkable that he would neglect her at the point of his death. Furthermore, the test of true religion that James set before his readers in chapter 1, verse 27, also reflects the teaching of the Old Testament Scriptures and even uses language that was drawn directly from them.

It is time, therefore, to go back and examine more thoroughly the foundation that the Lord laid for these patterns of conduct toward the widow in particular that he gave to Israel through his servant Moses. We have already noted the fact that the care of the widow is not based primarily on humanitarian considerations. Instead, there is a deeper vein to mine, which is rooted in the words and actions of the redeeming Lord of the covenant toward his people Israel. Included in the covenant are specific instructions regarding the treatment of the widow. Some of these passages have been mentioned already, but it is necessary to return to them and also consider other passages in order to feel the full force of the Old Testament instructions. Then we can appreciate their implications for understanding the New Testament practice regarding the widow and allow this knowledge to influence our own present-day actions.

The Sovereign Lord

The sovereign Lord of the covenant is the source of all the legislation regarding widows, not Moses or any of the subsequent kings of Israel. Moses made that plain.

> For the LORD your God is God of gods and Lord of lords, the great God, mighty and awesome, who shows no partiality nor takes a bribe. He administers justice for the fatherless and the widow, and loves the stranger, giving him food and clothing. (Deut. 10:17–18)

The character of God lies behind the way he said Israel was to treat those who were in specific need. He showed no partiality nor did he resort to bribery or other forms of injustice. His people were expected to be like him. Indeed, if they feared their Lord, then they would walk in all his ways; they would love him; they would serve him with all their heart and soul. This was what their redeemer Lord required of them (Deut. 10:12).

Therefore, the way they treated the widow was to be a direct expression of their love for God and their ready obedience to him. Thousands of years have passed since the sovereign Lord first spoke these words, but the principles remain for Christians today. In ministry to the widow, the church should be consciously reflecting the character of God himself and the compassion of the Lord Jesus Christ. We are called to administer justice for the widow, and neglect of this calling brings God's displeasure on us. This care is one of the ways to manifest the true colors of "pure and undefiled religion" (James 1:27), because it testifies to the character of the God who has redeemed us.

His Provision for the Widow

The aim of God's provision for the widow is to ensure a safety net exists for her. We have already seen that she was not to be exploited (Ex. 22:21–22, repeated in another form in Deut. 27:19). Additionally, her garment was not to be taken as a pledge (that is, as collateral for a loan), thus depriving her of warmth and clothing (Deut. 24:17). A specific explanation follows in verse 18 as the motivation to the Israelites. They were commanded to obey these provisions because they were once slaves in Egypt but had been redeemed from their bondage. The Lord was spelling out the implications of this deliverance. They were to act in a merciful manner toward the widow because *they* belonged to God and he had shown *them* mercy by redeeming them.

She was to be allowed to glean in the fields, the olive groves, and the vineyards. If someone accidentally left a sheaf of corn in the field, he was to leave it there specifically for the stranger, the fatherless, and the widow (Deut. 24:19–22). A similar reason to the one in verse 18 is given in verse 22. Remember, Boaz responded to this commandment of the Lord when he let Ruth glean in his fields. Notice also that obedience to such words was attended by the

Lord's blessings in all the work of their hands (24:19). And we saw that Boaz was not a disappointed man!

Furthermore, the tithes were to be shared with the widow (Deut. 14:28–29; 26:12–13), and provision was to be made for her at the principal religious feasts (Deut. 16:9–15). The establishment of the levirate law was intended to protect her, as we have seen in the case of Ruth. That law had in view both the provision of an heir for the land of a childless widow and also the provision of aid to her so that she became integrated into the normal life of the people of God (Deut. 25:5–10).

His Protection of the Widow

The Lord recognized that widows were vulnerable and therefore in need of protection. We have already seen that Isaiah and the other prophets rallied to the cause of exploited widows and exposed the wickedness of those who ill-treated them (Isa. 1:23; 10:1–3; Jer. 22:3; Ezek. 22:7; Mal. 3:5). Part of their ministry was to call their contemporaries to repentance and to redress the wrongs inflicted on these widows. The foundation for their ministry, though, was initially laid out in the legislation that the Lord gave to Moses.

There was no question that a widow was open to becoming a victim of the unscrupulous who had no fear of God in their hearts (see Ex. 22:22–23). Anyone who sought to take advantage of her in her poverty or her vulnerability could expect the Lord to act in vengeance. The Lord warned his people that he would not idly stand by, ignore the widow's pleas, and let the perpetrators of such injustice get away scot-free. He would act in order to punish those who exploited the widow. So careful was the Lord to protect the widow that even the boundaries of her property were his concern (Prov. 15:25).

The Distinctive Calling of Israel

Earlier we noted that God held similar concerns for the plight of the widow in other cultures and countries in the ancient world. However, there was something distinctive about Israel. That distinctiveness was rooted in theology and in redemption. Israel had once been a powerless nation, enslaved and harshly treated by her Egyptian overlords. The Lord had shown them mercy and delivered them from their bondage. He had redeemed them—"I bore you on eagles' wings and brought you to Myself" (Ex. 19:4).

Israel was called to imitate this pattern of compassion and kindness that they themselves had experienced. They were not to forget their former years in slavery nor their present status as God's redeemed people. When they forgot those years of slavery and lost their own identity, then they became like the other nations and began to mistreat the widows among them. God identified himself as the legal defender of the widow (Ps. 68:5), her guardian, and the guardian of her inherited property (as well as the father of orphans). Remarkably, so extensive was the concern of the Lord for widows that in Jeremiah 49:11 even widows from outside Israel (in this case Edom) could trust in the God of Israel. The stories of Ruth the Moabitess and the widow of Zarephath had proved this was the case.

The Implications for the Church of Christ Today

The details of God's provision for widows are not the same today, but the principles remain. The church is surely called to imitate the Lord whom we serve. We have been the beneficiaries of his mercy; he has redeemed us from sin and not dealt with us as our sins deserve. He has not dealt harshly with us and consequently calls us to demonstrate his compassion openly in this fallen world. A ministry to widows is a vital part of that calling. We are not to neglect them by ignoring them or by leaving their care to somebody else. We are certainly not to deal harshly with them and take advantage of them. It is a clear biblical teaching and principle that if the fear of God is firmly planted in our hearts, then we will care for the widow.

Additionally, there are far fewer orphans in the Western world than in former days, but they should not be neglected either. There is scope for Christians to take initiatives by providing foster homes and by adopting children into their families. Abortion is widespread in the Western world. It is possible (though not easy to arrange) for Christians to provide a home for unwanted children who would otherwise be needlessly aborted.

Care for widows remains high on the church's agenda and will continue to be until the return of Christ. Our responsibilities should be more evident as the truth of the Scriptures is unfolded in the next chapters.

6

The Significance of the Old Covenant Provisions

Before turning to the teaching of the New Testament Scriptures in more detail, this chapter will consider why the cause of the widow, together with the orphan and the stranger, was repeatedly brought before the attention of the nation of Israel. As we have already seen, although similar laws have been discovered among other ancient nations, Israel was distinctive. God specifically summoned his people to care and provide for the needy. Their sovereign Lord had come to their aid when they had no strength of their own and redeemed them from bondage in Egypt. In the same way, they were to come to the aid of the widow.

This same theme found in many of the books of the Old Testament is also expressed in the last book, Malachi. When the nation forgot God, he responded. Part of the ministry of the messenger of the covenant, the forerunner of the Messiah (as well as that of the Messiah himself) was to bring divine judgment on those who "exploit wage earners and widows and orphans" (Mal. 3:1–6). Why was this subject given such prominence in the Law and the Prophets? Remember, we have already suggested that these provisions cannot be adequately explained on humanitarian grounds alone.

God's Provisions for Widows Tell Us about the Character of God

The covenant provisions that pervade the Old Testament Scriptures display the character of the Lord. Even though widows are not mentioned in Psalm 113, they were surely included among the poor and needy who are described. He who is "high above all nations" also "humbles Himself to behold the things that are in the heavens and in the earth" (vv. 4, 6). Like an oriental king, the Lord mercifully reached down to those in the dust and on the ash heap and exalted them, treating them as royalty. He was their helper and redeemer, just as he was the redeemer of Israel. While the psalm principally has Hannah in view (1 Samuel 1–2), it also has a much wider horizon—for example, the mercy the Lord displayed to Ruth and the widow of Zarephath! He reached down to them to exalt them by giving Ruth a husband, a home, and children, and by raising up the widow's dead son. By displaying his mercy and his power, he and he alone brought joy when bitterness and despair threatened to overwhelm them.

Aloofness is hardly a charge anyone could bring against the sovereign Lord. His fatherlike character is also reflected in the character of his Son, for Psalm 113 also anticipates the wonder of the gospel.

> For you know the grace of our Lord Jesus Christ, that though He was rich, yet for your sakes He became poor, that you through His poverty might become rich. (2 Cor. 8:9)

This verse encapsulates the great downward and upward sweep of the gospel that Psalm 113 expresses. One commentator tersely notes, "There is plainly much more than rhetoric in the question of verse 5, 'Who is like the Lord our God?'"[6]

It is also worth pointing out that 2 Corinthians 8:9 occurs in the context of the church's practical ministry to the saints in need, and it expresses the motive that Paul set before the Corinthians to inspire their generosity. Those who would be the beneficiaries of this generosity among the Judean Christians were undoubtedly widows.

God's Provisions for Widows Tell Us about the Conduct of God

Flowing on naturally from the consideration of his character, these covenant provisions reflect the conduct of the Lord. They show us the divine scale of values and his ethic—who is significant in his eyes—together with the kind of behavior that he finds acceptable and requires toward those he identifies. He sets the standards of goodness, kindness, and mercy. He displays righteousness. Israel was to mirror that conduct. As we have seen, when God's ethic was forgotten, it was the poor and needy who suffered most as a result of human unrighteousness.

That ethic was carried over into the New Testament church and was expressed not only in the conduct of the Lord Jesus Christ toward widows but also in the teaching and practice of the church, as we shall see. Therefore, the twenty-first-century church should follow the same pattern. We live in a world dominated by advanced information technology. Social media continues to grow at an explosive rate. However, sin still creates havoc in the lives of everyone on this planet. Since the fall of the human race, mankind remains helpless prey to the evil influence of sin and Satan. Advanced technology is no substitute for the redeeming power of God in Jesus Christ that so richly demonstrates his compassion and his love.

We live in a world of self-indulgent individualism, a world that tends to be dominated by powerful politicians, military leaders, rich businesspeople, elite sports stars, and a variety of entertainers. Such men and women are hardly ever out of the public eye. The attention the media gives them reveals that the ethical priorities of the world are very different from divine priorities. The poor and the needy are passed by and tend to be forgotten. The church of Christ must continue to be different and godlike by continually being doers of the Word and demonstrating "pure and undefiled religion" (James 1:27).

God's Provisions for Widows Point Us to the Way of Salvation

These provisions also point to the salvation that the Lord Jesus Christ brought when he came preaching the gospel of the kingdom of God. In the synagogue at Nazareth, he effectively told the startled congregation that he was the Messiah, anointed with the Spirit and appointed to preach the gospel to the poor in fulfilment of the prophet Isaiah's words (Isa. 49:8–9; 61:1–2). The passage clearly is not limited to those who are actually widows and orphans. The picture is much bigger and richer. The truth is that *God* saves sinners.

As with the poor, the widow, the orphan, and the alien, sinners are destitute and helpless. They possess no wealth or strength of their own. They cannot extricate themselves from their grief, their guilt, or their distress. Instead, in order to be saved, sinners are cast upon the mercy of God and his Son, who came to give us life more abundantly (John 10:9–10). What we need first and foremost is salvation from our sins. The way God deals with the widow and others who are poor and needy depicts the way he deals with sinners. Like Ruth, sinners come to take refuge under the shadow of his wings. They are also stripped of their pride, like Naaman the Syrian army commander. For him, great and famous as he was, God's way of healing him was a painful but necessary lesson of his own helplessness (2 Kings 5). He was not cured of his leprosy until he was made to see that he must wash in the Jordan seven times, just as Elisha had told him. God alone could cure him.

God's Provisions for Widows Point Us to Permanent Spiritual Relationships

Finally, without for one moment minimizing the grief and sorrows experienced in becoming a widow, we can say that—spiritually speaking—no one who is a Christian is ever a widow, an orphan, or a stranger. Every Christian is united to Christ by faith. The Lord Jesus Christ came as a Bridegroom for his bride, the church (Eph. 5:25–32). We are married to Christ and there is a marriage feast to be enjoyed in the future (Rev. 19:7–9; cf. Matt. 8:11).

This is something which is invariably very hard for a recently bereaved widow to believe. To draw comfort from such biblical teaching seems impossible. A heavy cloud of grief hangs over her head. She may be paralyzed by shock, especially if her husband died suddenly and unexpectedly. Pastors need to handle such a situation with much care and sensitivity, and probably hold back certain counsel until a more appropriate time.

Eventually, a widow should be able to enter more fully into the joy of knowing she has a heavenly husband and that she is also an adopted daughter of God, a child of God with a Father in heaven who loves and cares for her. By dying on Calvary's cross, the Lord Jesus established those permanent family ties. Furthermore, no Christian is cut off from the supplies of strength and spiritual succor, for Christ has promised that he will not leave us as orphans (John 14:8). He is our Great High Priest, who is thoroughly acquainted with our weaknesses, who has been tempted in all points like us, and who is yet without sin. All believers, widows included, are urged to "come boldly to the throne of grace, that we may obtain mercy and find grace to help in time of need" (Heb. 4:14–16).

The church of Jesus Christ is called to preach the gospel to a lost and guilty world. Sinners stand—spiritually speaking—widowed, orphaned, and destitute outside of the family of God. Preachers are sent to turn them "from darkness to light, and from the power of Satan to God, that they may receive forgiveness of sins and an inheritance among those who are sanctified by faith in [Jesus Christ]" (Acts 26:18).

We continue to live in this fallen world, however, where sin and death are ever present. Until the Lord Jesus Christ appears and brings in his eternal kingdom, the church will be called to "visit orphans and widows in their trouble" (James 1:27) and to mirror the character and conduct of the God who has saved his people through the Lord Jesus Christ. With this in mind, we turn in the next chapter to the New Testament Scriptures and the teaching and practice of Christ and the early church.

7

The Character and Conduct of Christ

We drew attention in an earlier chapter to the compassion Christ displayed toward his widowed mother. In this chapter, we will consider the character and the conduct of Christ toward widows. This can only be fully appreciated in the context of the Old Testament Scriptures, which we have already addressed. Sometimes his ministry and conduct is discussed as if it were isolated from that context, but as we provide the biblical rationale for the church's ministry toward widows in particular, it is important to see that there is a consistent theme running through the entire body of Scripture.

The Faithfulness of Anna

It was Anna, the widow and prophetess, who was privileged to see and testify about the infant Redeemer (Luke

2:36–38). At the age of eighty-four, she was advanced in years, but she had faithfully served God in the temple with fasting and prayer night and day. As a widow without family responsibilities, she had devoted herself completely to the service of God. It was she, together with others not highly regarded in the eyes of the world, who spoke of the birth of Christ to those who looked for redemption in Jerusalem. The fact that the birth of Christ was proclaimed by such a lady tells us that it was not beneath the dignity of the Lord to be spoken of in this manner by one who was among the poorest of the poor.

The Parable of the Persistent Widow

Some of the hardships facing the widow in this world are reflected in the parable Jesus told in Luke 18:1–8. Here was a widow who kept demanding that her case be heard and that justice be upheld by an unprincipled and wicked judge. Jesus used her situation to urge his followers to persist in prayer, crying out to God day and night, knowing that he will bring about justice and eventually redress all wrongs suffered by his elect in this life.

The roots of this parable are embedded not only in the realities of living in a world where there is exploitation and unjust judgment, but also in the Law and the Prophets. It is abundantly clear where Christ's sympathies lay and what shaped his parable. Behind this story lies the reality that God is the ultimate defender of the widow and that her cries reach his ears. The unjust judge cared neither for God nor man (v. 4). He could not have been more unlike the Lord in his attitude toward this widow (cf. Ex. 22:22; Deut. 24:17). By implication, Christ endorses all that the Old Testament Scriptures taught.

Christ's Condemnation of the Scribes and Pharisees

Furthermore, in keeping with the warnings of Moses and with the reproofs of the prophets, the Lord Jesus Christ also exposed the scribes and Pharisees for their practice of devouring widows' houses. The same condemnation is found in identical form in three of the Gospels (Matt. 23:14; Mark 12:40; Luke 20:47). The widows of Christ's day were evidently subject to financial exploitation by the Jewish religious leaders. Not only were those leaders guilty of covetousness, but the word "devour" dramatically portrays their unscrupulous practice and abuse. The scribes (most of whom were Pharisees) were not wealthy and were not paid for the work they did. Consequently, many well-to-do people placed their financial resources at the disposal of the scribes, and such a situation was open to abuse.

When Christ condemned the conduct of the scribes and Pharisees, he was probably thinking of the way some of them sponged on the hospitality of people with limited means, such as widows. Some widows were rich, however, and by gaining their confidence, scribes could enrich themselves under the cover of piety. One commentator mentions that scribes served as consultants in estate planning for widows. If they were driven by impure motives, it would not be difficult for them to convince lonely, susceptible widows that their money and property should either be given to the scribe for his holy work or to the temple for its holy ministries. Either way the scribe stood to make personal gains.[7] Such hypocrisy drew out righteous indignation and condemnation from the lips of the incarnate Son of God.

Church leaders today are no less immune to the same temptations as the scribes and Pharisees. The potential exploitation of a richer widow was probably one reason behind Paul's insistence that elders must not be "greedy for money" (1 Tim. 3:3; Titus 1:7). Hypocrisy can fester in any heart that professes to be religious. Some widows are more vulnerable than others and can be more easily deceived. Safeguards must be put in place by churches to prevent such deception, and a working system of financial accountability should be implemented. If monies change hands without appropriate precautions being established in a church, accusations of financial impropriety will likely follow. The integrity of the church or individuals in the church will not only be questioned but may come under severe scrutiny in the law courts.

Christ's Commendation of the Poor Widow

In both Mark's and Luke's Gospel the condemnation of the scribes and Pharisees' conduct is immediately followed by the commendation of the widow who placed her two mites into the temple treasury (Mark 12:41–44; Luke 21:1–4). Clearly both of them intend to highlight the contrast between the spiritual poverty of the scribes and Pharisees and the wholehearted devotion of the widow in spite of her material poverty.

The Lord Jesus Christ observed not merely the act of giving but the manner of giving. His eye falls on one particular financially destitute widow, literally, "one poor widow" (Mark 12:42). Many others would perhaps have ignored her or regarded her as insignificant in comparison with the rich who were noisily putting their contributions into the trumpet-shaped chests. Calling his disciples to himself, Jesus proceeded to tell them that her two mites (tiny copper coins) were proportionately larger than the gifts of those who gave out of their abundance. She had put in all she had, and in his eyes, it was as if she had given a gift more valuable than gold. She had given to God her last means of support, for she had entrusted herself entirely to his care.

Widows, therefore, should never be ignored or underestimated. This widow had done a noble thing in the eyes of Christ. He reversed the standards by which people are judged. It is all too easy for the church to ape the attitude of the world. To be like Christ, however, demands that we take note of the widow and not hastily dismiss her or her piety. That standard is yet another reason why James spoke of true religion as having regard for the widow in her troubles.

8

Christ and Elijah

The Lord Jesus Christ was no stranger to the prophet Elijah. On the Mount of Transfiguration, Elijah and Moses talked with him (Matt. 17:3). Also, in the earliest days of his ministry in the synagogue in Nazareth, Jesus told the assembled congregation about Elijah (Luke 4:25–26). There he reminded them how Elijah had been sent to one specific widow in Zarephath in the region of Sidon rather than to the many widows in Israel. In chapter 5 of this book, we considered the plight of this particular widow and how the Lord provided for her needs by raising her son to life in answer to Elijah's prayers. Similarly, the raising of the widow of Nain's son from the dead in Luke 7:11–17 reminds us of the miracle Elijah performed for the widow of Zarephath.

The Plight of the Widow of Nain

In the Gospels we read of three people whom Jesus raised from the dead: Lazarus, the brother of Mary and Martha;

the daughter of Jairus, the synagogue ruler; and the unnamed son of the widow of Nain. Like Naomi and the widow of Zarephath, this woman's situation was tragic. Her son had been cut down by death in the prime of life. Luke recorded her plight tenderly. He was "the only son of his mother; and she was a widow" (7:12). He was her one remaining source of protection and financial support. Any hope of perpetuating the family line had vanished with his death. She had already experienced one trial in the death of her husband and had perhaps raised her son without a man's help and influence. Jesus and his disciples met the somber funeral procession as their paths crossed just outside the gates of the city of Nain. At the head of the crowd a few men were carrying the covered body of the young man. Behind them was a grieving mother, together with a large crowd, which probably included hired mourners and musicians. Such a procession could hardly be ignored.

The Goodness of Christ in High Definition

Luke later records a significant summary of Christ's earthly ministry in Acts 10:38. "God anointed Jesus of Nazareth with the Holy Spirit and with power, who went about doing good . . . for God was with Him." Outside the gates of Nain, we see the goodness of the Lord Jesus Christ in high definition. As soon as he saw the widow, his heart went out to her in godlike compassion. Immediately, he knew the reasons for her tears. He spoke a kind word of command

and told her to stop weeping. He came near and touched the open coffin, halting the procession to the burial ground as he did so.

On other occasions Jesus received requests for help. This time there was no such cry. All he saw and heard was enough for him to respond spontaneously, for his heart throbbed with compassion. The widow and her dead son were helpless in the face of sin and death. But, in an act of divine pity joined with divine power, he spoke to the dead man and commanded him to arise. The young man sat up and began to speak, much to the astonishment of the crowd in the funeral procession. They were afraid but at the same time realized that this was no ordinary event. Perhaps remembering what Elijah had done many years before, they were ready to declare Jesus to be a great prophet and that God had visited his people.

There is one further observation to be made, however, which once again displays the tenderness and sensitivity of the Lord toward this widow. Not only did he raise her son from the dead and give him life, but in verse 15 Luke records that "he *presented* him to his mother." The words are almost identical to those in 1 Kings 17:23 and 2 Kings 4:36. It was a wonderful moment. No promises were extracted from her and no conditions were laid down by Jesus. It was sheer divine mercy and power. It was a demonstration of divine grace. It was a mother who needed her only son to protect and provide for her, and Jesus provided this need willingly. It was the same kind of goodness and care he would later show toward his own mother, providing for and protecting her by entrusting her into the hands of John.

This story about the widow of Nain tells us that Jesus Christ is able to save us from death. She was a weak and desolate widow. He was the mighty Savior. He restored the son to his mother. What Jesus did for the young man, he will one day do for all those who die in Christ, "For if we believe that Jesus died and rose again, even so God will bring with Him those who sleep in Jesus" (1 Thess. 4:14).

The church cannot show the same kind of power as that shown by Christ, but—in keeping with everything that is commanded in the covenant provisions of the Old Testament—the church is called to act toward the widow with Christlike compassion. His heart went out to her in her trouble. To ignore the needs of widows would be to show contempt for God, to fail to love our neighbors (in this case needy widows). Such neglect would soon become a blight on the testimony of the church. Everything that we see in the life of Christ confirms what we have already seen in the Old Testament. The church scarcely needs more warrant for ministering to widows.

9

Widows, the Church in Jerusalem, and Deacons

James defined the essence of true religion as showing compassion to the poor and needy, particularly identifying the widow and the orphan in their trouble. He was not a lone voice in the New Testament church. In the early days of the church, it was clear that special provision was made for the widow (Acts 6:1–7). Paul wrote to Timothy in Ephesus much later after the recorded events in the book of Acts. He included clear instructions about the care of the widow, urging younger widows to remarry, while those who were "widows really" were to be cared for by the church (1 Tim. 5:3–16). Given what we have seen in the law of Moses, in the Old Testament Prophets especially, and in the example and the teaching of Christ himself, it would be very strange if there was nothing further by way of example and teaching about the care of widows in the apostolic Scriptures.

Tensions in Jerusalem

As the church in Jerusalem continued to grow, problems arose. There was persecution and opposition almost from the very beginning. Then within the community of disciples, the hypocrisy of Ananias and Sapphira was exposed. That event may have been partly related to the care of widows. According to Acts 4:34–35, there was no one in the church who lacked anything. Lands and houses were sold by those who were in a position to do so, and the resulting funds were given to the apostles to use in the church. They then "distributed to each as anyone had need." It is reasonable to conclude that this included widows, just as the later collection for the Judean saints mentioned by Paul in 2 Corinthians 8–9 did.

Social and cultural tensions arose in the church in Jerusalem. There were two groups—the "purer" Jewish element who spoke Aramaic and were deeply immersed in Jewish culture, and the Hellenistic Jews who had adopted the Greek language and customs. The latter began to murmur and perhaps even complain that their widows were being overlooked. An appearance of partiality seemed to have entered the church, with the implication that the daily distribution of food was not being carried out in a fair manner.

The precise circumstances are not clear. Luke gives no indication that partiality had taken deep root in the church. Perhaps the apparent preferential treatment was not deliberate but more a reflection of the increasing problem of caring for so many widows. Whatever the actual reasons, realizing that something needed to be done to prevent a serious division in the church, the apostles acted, not only to prevent division from happening but also to ensure that the widows were provided for adequately.

Establishing Deacons

The apostles realized that they could not take primary responsibility for carrying out the task because they would then be distracted from their duties of prayer and the ministry of the Word. As a result, seven men were chosen as deacons. They were qualified for the task: they were men of good reputation, full of the Holy Spirit, and wise (v. 3). There are differences of opinion over the interpretation of this passage. Personally, I am persuaded that these seven men were appointed as deacons in order to reflect the compassion of Christ. We saw that in the days of the old covenant, God undertook to defend and to relieve widows. The Jerusalem church was not therefore creating something new; they were continuing Old Testament principles and practice.

It is important to realize, however, that it was not the creation of the diaconate that led to the care of the widows in the church. They were already being provided for from the very beginning (Acts 2:44–45). These seven men were appointed in order to ensure that the duty was carried out fully and fairly. We have seen that the Scriptures require God's people to show mercy and meet the widows' needs. A widow, therefore, has a God-given right to expect the church to visit her in her troubles, to relieve her, as well as to comfort her. No widow should ever be in a position in which she is neglected and her needs ignored.

This is very important because, by being cared for in the prescribed way, a widow can continue to live among the people of God and continue to serve Christ according to her abilities. For a widow, the worship, the life, and the ministry of the church remain central in the will of God despite all the changes that have taken place as a result of the death of her husband.

The Role of Deacons Today

In the Western world the care of widows is usually seen as the duty of the state. That is not the biblical perspective at all. We have established that the care of widows, carried out by the people of God, must be much more than a humanitarian response. There are theological reasons for demonstrating care for widows, not least that the church of God has been redeemed by Christ. He has reached down to us in our desperate need as lost and guilty sinners and saved us by his mercy and grace. In response, the church is to reflect the character and conduct of God in her care of others who are needy, not the least widows.

Too often the role of deacons is not considered or undertaken from this perspective. In the light of what we have seen, should not deacons perceive themselves as Christ's ministers of mercy, with a duty to demonstrate the compassion of their Lord? The apostles drew a clear line of demarcation in terms of the priorities that belonged to them and to deacons. That is not to say that elders should never do the work of deacons—that would mean that they do not have to display the compassion of Christ to those in need. It does mean, however, that the primary responsibility for the practical care of widows falls on the shoulders of the deacons of the church. Therefore, they should be taking the first steps to visit widows in their trouble, mobilizing others in the church if necessary, rather than waiting for the elders to take the initiative.

Part of the reason for writing this book is to stress that the ongoing care of widows should have a priority on the agenda of churches, and of deacons in particular. Repeatedly, I have come across situations where widows have been forgotten within a few weeks of the funeral of their husband and left to fend for themselves as best as they are able. Who is going to speak up on their behalf? Given the clear teaching of the Word of God, can we remain silent?

10

"Really Widows"

In 1 Timothy 5 Paul dealt with life in the church and gave precise instructions to Timothy about how he was to treat older men, younger men, older women, younger women, widows, and how to honor elders. The longest section in that chapter relates to the care of widows, verses 3–16, and in particular to those who are "really widows" (v. 3). Paul's principal concern was that the church should fulfill its duties by providing relief for these women. There were other issues and problems, however, relating to widows in Ephesus. The situation was very different from that facing the church in Jerusalem.

Provision for Widows by Their Families

All widows need the spiritual comfort of the church's ministry and the warmth of true friendship and fellowship, but not all widows have identical circumstances. Not every widow requires the financial support of the church. The Lord entrusted his mother to John, and he took her into his own home. God provides for some widows through their extended family. To provide care for a widow is a matter of Christian obedience for her children and grandchildren (1 Tim. 5:4). That duty needs to be a matter of public teaching in many situations today. It would be optimistic to assume that everyone will conclude that this is their Christian duty.

Paul makes it very clear that if a widow has grown-up children, they owe her a debt. In God's eyes, caring for an aging, widowed mother is a small return for the fifteen to twenty years during which she looked after and raised her children. God requires such care: it is something good and acceptable to him. In some circumstances it may not be possible for this to happen, but the church is to be wise and discerning and then take appropriate steps. For example, what should a church do if the widow has unbelieving children who refuse to take care of their widowed mother? In other cases, the onset of advanced dementia may make the task of caring for a mother impossible.

A few years ago the media in the USA drew attention to the practice of "granny dumping." Elderly and sometimes sick mothers were just left at the door of hospitals for others to assume the financial and social responsibility of their care. In a world where sin and selfishness have taken root in the human heart, it is not unusual to find widows neglected because of hardness of heart and a lack of love for parents on the part of their children. The apostle Paul did not mince words. If anyone fails to provide for his own, especially those of his own household, he has denied the faith and is to be regarded as worse than an unbeliever (v. 8). True religion begins at home. To deny the faith is effectively to deny the God who has saved you in his mercy and kindness. To fail to provide for a widowed mother when it is within your capacity to do so should be unthinkable for a Christian.

The Real Widow

Paul's burden was to ensure that women of God, who were very vulnerable and needy because they had no family members to provide for and protect them, were cared for by the church. These were ladies well known for their godliness. They trusted in God as the defender of widows and knew what it was to cast themselves on God in prayer. Paul outlines specific good works that must characterize such a widow—she has brought up children, she has been hospitable and lodged strangers, she has ministered to the saints, and she has relieved the afflicted. In short, she is known for having diligently pursued every good work (v. 10).

There are different opinions about the precise meaning of verses 9 and 10. Some are persuaded that Paul is setting out the high standards required for widows who are going to serve in the church and become recognized women workers, perhaps deaconesses.[8] He even sets a minimum age of sixty in order to be classed as a real widow and also adds she must be the wife of one man (v. 9). Others take these same verses and say that they describe the kind of widow who is worthy of the church's full care and support.

It may be possible to combine this passage with what Paul writes to Titus, in chapter 2, about the work of older women, whether they are widows or not. There he outlined a number of duties that are the essence of godliness. In particular the older woman was to be a good example and teacher to younger women, admonishing them to love their husbands and their children, so that they were discreet, chaste homemakers, focused on good, and obedient to their own husbands. In this way, he concludes, the Word of God will not be blasphemed (vv. 3–5). If we put this passage alongside 1 Timothy 5:9–10, we have a blueprint for the character and work of an older godly woman in the church of Christ. A widow may have distinct new opportunities to abound in good works because she has the scope of a free woman to serve Christ (cf. 1 Cor. 7:34–35).

The Example of Dorcas

It may be that Dorcas falls into this category of an older godly woman, though Scripture does not specifically say she was a widow (Acts 9:36–43). Her example does indicate, however, that the church in Joppa was also ministering to widows in need. Dorcas was described as being "full of good works and charitable deeds" (v. 36). When she died, it was the widows who were weeping the most. Her ministry was held in high regard by them. She had been a talented seamstress, making tunics and garments for them. When Peter came, he prayed and raised her from the dead. Then he called together both the saints *and* the widows and presented her alive. We may assume that Dorcas resumed her good works and charitable deeds, much to the joy of the widows in Joppa.

Young Widows

Paul also has some clear instructions for young widows in 1 Timothy 5. Some were mishandling the situation. Instead of casting their cares on God and learning to display contentment and godliness, they were casting off their first faith, becoming not only idle but also gossips and busybodies (v. 13). So serious was the situation in Ephesus that some had already turned after Satan. Paul told Timothy that young widows should, if possible, remarry, bear children, and manage their homes. In that way, they would silence the reproach of Satan. Such directions would not be easy to implement.

The Lord Jesus Christ required the church to exercise discernment in the care and support of widows among them. The elders in the church together with the deacons should assume those responsibilities. Clearly, it was no minor matter because the reputations of the church and the Lord Jesus Christ were at stake. Church discipline might have been involved as some widows became devoted to pleasure, showing very little concern for godliness (v. 6). Only godly widows were to be honored. They alone were to be supported and shown respect by the church.

"Honor" (v. 3) holds the idea of meeting particular needs, including financial needs. Therefore, no widow should expect to be able to sponge off the church, and no family with the means of caring for their widowed mother should expect the church to meet her needs.

Every church, together with her elders and deacons, clearly has responsibilities to discharge with regard to believing widows. The question of widows who are not believers and are outside the body of Christ is another matter. The Lord showed mercy to Ruth and to the widow of Zarephath. If the Lord first showed mercy to us when we were aliens "from the commonwealth of Israel . . . having no hope and without God in the world" (Eph. 2:12), then we must surely cast our net wider than believing widows. The church is called to preach the gospel not only to widows but to all men, for God our Savior desires that "all men . . . be saved and . . . come to the knowledge of the truth" (1 Tim. 2:4).

Part 2

Pastoral Application

Brian Croft

11

Minister the Word

There is so much pastors, deacons, church leaders, and other caregivers can do to care physically and emotionally for widows in meaningful ways. Much of the next part of this book focuses on meeting those needs in creative, unique, and significant ways. But before we dig into the trenches of this noble work, it is essential that we highlight the primary role of a pastor in caring for a widow. This comes through a careful and thoughtful ministry of the Word of God.

The entire first half of this book was not just to inform you of God's desire to care for the widow in these inescapable examples and imperatives from Scripture, but to equip pastors and other caregivers with the tools to offer life-giving ministry to these hurting ladies. We must prepare for this kind of ministry and, with God's help, then provide the spiritual comfort God intends with his divine Word to widows in particular.

Prepare to Minister the Word

Never underestimate the intuition of a widow. She will often know through our manner if we have come out of love or obligation. This is the first heart issue we must honestly assess. It is an easy trap to fall into, especially for pastors. We begin to think that visiting is part of the job for which the church has hired us. Pastors must make a special effort to be sure they are visiting a widow out of love and care, not merely obligation. Curtis Thomas, a seasoned American pastor of over forty years, writes in regard to hospital visits to our people:

> Our visits should never appear only as professional duties. If the patient perceives that we are there only to carry out our responsibility, rather than having a genuine concern for him or her, our visit can do more harm than good.[9]

These wise words should be applied in the care of the widow whether in a hospital or in the comforts of her own home.

We must also prepare our hearts for what we might see and experience. The loneliness and grief a widow could be experiencing may be very intense depending upon how recently her husband passed away. We need to prepare for uncomfortable moments that could come from uncontrollable weeping, physical suffering that can accompany deep levels of grief, or simply the hard theological questions of

Why? that we cannot answer. The more prepared we are for these moments, the better we will discern how best to care for each hurting saint of the Lord seeking his care through us.

While in her home, we should prepare our hearts to discern any physical care that might be needed. We have trained the deacons in my church to visit widows with the intent to ask what needs to be fixed in the home or what piece of furniture needs to be moved that she is unable to do on her own. The dilemma in Acts 6 was to address the physical need of the widows who were being neglected. Never underestimate the valuable service to a widow when you seek to care for her physical needs. The best way to determine what those needs might be (other than simply to ask) is to consider what tasks her husband would have handled if he were still alive and in the home. Addressing these physical needs could touch the heart of a widow in ways you may not realize and prepare her to receive the spiritual nourishment of God's Word you have come to minister.

Provide the Ministry of the Word

The most important task of a pastor is to bring spiritual care and encouragement to a widow. It is important that pastors see it as their responsibility to show a widow God's care for her. Over a period of time, a pastor needs to demonstrate that God provides this care by teaching her much of the material covered in the first part of this book. Although instructing the widow in God's care and provision for her requires much sensitivity to timing and approach, a pastor also needs to be careful to actively share this material with her and not focus only on her physical needs. Pastors best accomplish spiritual care through prayer and the ministry of the Word that is intentionally focused on God's desire and care for the widow.

Have a few passages ready when you visit that you think might speak into the loneliness and despair a certain widow would be experiencing. Ask questions about how she is doing, and her answers will give you guidance on what word from Scripture would bring her comfort and in what direction to pray. It is helpful to think through these in categories. Here are five areas with passage examples that may be helpful in a variety of situations:

Situation	Bible Passage
Comfort to widows specifically	Psalms 23; 28; 34; 46; 62; 68:5; 113; Jer. 49:11; Heb. 4:14–16
Reflection of God's intentional care for widows	Deut. 16:11; Ruth 1–4; 1 Kings 17; Ps. 146:9; Lam. 1:1–2; Luke 7:12–13; Acts 6:1–7; 1 Tim. 5:1–10
Succinct gospel presentation	John 11:25–26; Rom. 5:6–11; 2 Cor. 5:17–21; Eph. 2:1–10

Situation	Bible Passage
The purpose of suffering for the believer	2 Cor. 12:7–9; James 1:2–4; 1 Pet. 1:6–7; 4:12–19
The reality and hope of eternity with Christ	John 10:27–30; 14:1–3; Phil. 1:21–23; 1 Pet. 1:3–5

Having a few passages in mind will allow you to be better equipped for the unexpected. Read part 1 of this book again if you are unclear of the ways these rich passages affirm God's passionate desire to care for widows. Don't forget your Bible. Whatever passage you choose for that moment, pray in line with the truths of that passage. This practice will reiterate the truths from Scripture you have just read and will keep a singular focus on what you hope the hurting widow retains after you have gone.

There is much we can do as we visit a widow—talk with her, see what her needs are, and try to meet them—but our calling and task from God is to minister God's grace through his Word and prayer. Go with this task as your primary goal, but don't rush into it too quickly. Take time to prepare your heart. Sit quietly and allow the God of all comfort through his life-giving Word to minister to your heart, mind, and soul before you go to care for others with the Word. God will bless your effort to prepare your own heart so that you might more effectively reach the heart of the widow with the power of the Spirit working through God's Word.

12

Equip the Church

This book is not just for pastors. Though we had pastors on our minds through much of its development, this work is intended to have a much broader purpose. It is also to be used deliberately to train and equip the people of your congregation in this task. It is to call deacons (Acts 6:1–7) to look for the needs of widows in the congregation and lead the charge to meet those needs. Our prayer is that pastors will not only be challenged by the exhortation to care for widows personally but that you will also be convicted to call your deacons to action and to train your people to follow them and do likewise. Before we dive into the specifics of meeting the physical and emotional needs of widows, here are some ways pastors can effectively teach, train, and motivate deacons, other church leaders, and caregivers in your congregation to see the value in caring for the widows within your local church.

Exhort through Preaching

As you are committed to preaching the Bible, look for those points of application that serve as exhortations to love, care for, and serve widows in your church. Regardless of the passage in the Bible you are preaching on a particular week, you will find a sovereign God who rules over the affliction and suffering of people. You will see God's glory displayed in his people caring for those in need for the sake of the gospel. This is one reason why expositional preaching is the most helpful steady diet for a local church. As you preach through books of the Bible, you are more likely to be confronted with texts that allow this type of instruction.

There is nothing wrong with making this biblical topic of widows, orphans, and the poor the basis for a short sermon series, however, when it would seem appropriate. Regardless of how you teach your congregation about caring for widows—whether through a short sermon series or through regular application in your expositional sermons—the preaching of the Word of God is what gives life to the church, and it is where we are able to exhort with authority to the entire body what is most important. This book's purpose is to demonstrate the unique biblical call to the church of Jesus Christ to engage in this task. Show that the care of widows is a priority by exhorting your people to do so through your public preaching.

Pray for Widows in Public Gatherings

Praying the never-ending prayer list when the church gathers can turn into a meaningless, painful mantra. This is not what we are proposing. We are encouraging you to pick certain widows by name in your church to highlight through public prayer for the purpose of informing and teaching your congregation about their circumstances and how best to care for them. Praying for these often-forgotten saints informs the congregation of what is going on, and it also allows you to teach your congregation of their needs and how practically to care for them through the way you pray publicly.

When you pray, pray specific biblical truths. Praise God for his sovereign power over death and the pain of separation from our loved ones. Thank God for the hope we have of resurrection one day because of Christ, even in the face of deep loss. Exalt our Savior Jesus Christ, who ministers grace and mercy in our greatest times of need. Rejoice in the promise from God that he will never leave or forsake us and that it extends to even the loneliest of widows. Pray for healing if it be God's will to heal a physically hurting widow. Pray for the gospel to be known in the lives of these ladies who are suffering as Christ is magnified in their weakness. Then, pray that as a local church the gospel would be seen in our faithful care of these precious saints. Seize the public gatherings of the church to pray for these ladies and their needs because these moments are not only wonderful to teach, motivate, and equip, but there is also great power in corporate intercession.

Inform Your People Regularly

Willing church members are more likely to serve widows in the church if they know what is going on and where to go. It can be very discouraging for someone who wants to help but does not know how to gather the appropriate information. Create a system within your local church so that members can be informed and updated regularly as circumstances develop and change. Bulletins and prayer chains have been an effective way to get the word out in the past and can still be useful now. Churchwide e-mails appear to be the trend for the future.

Whatever the method, be committed to keeping your people updated on not just the circumstances of widows, so your congregation knows how to pray better, but also on the information they need to go and physically visit and care for widows. Below are just a few specific details that are helpful for those in your congregation who are more detached from the daily grind of pastoral labor:

- Where the widows are located and their current health circumstances
- Whether the widows want visitors and when
- When did the widows lose their spouses
- Something that church members can go and do for the widows

Busy church members can find endless reasons not to bother with caring for widows. Let us not allow "being uninformed" serve as an excuse.

Lead by Example

We cannot expect our people to be faithful in this task if we are not. Just because this is a very obvious truth about our entire lives as pastors, it does not give us the luxury of dismissing its needed weight in this area. We can preach on caring for widows, we can pray in every public gathering for them by name, we can give a detailed assessment of the daily needs of widows, but if we are not engaged in visiting these ladies ourselves and our congregations are not affected by our efforts, we have failed. If we are not challenging our deacons to lead in this kind of ministry as described in the New Testament, others will not follow. A soldier is more willing to follow his general into battle than simply to charge upon the general's command from a distant post, and this is true of pastors and their people. Fellow pastors, we must not only visit but model a burden for the widows in our church for our people to follow. We must be willing to delegate and empower deacons to meet certain needs as they arise. We must model a great faith in our sovereign God and a tender fellowship with our Savior in these moments, knowing he works all things for his own glory and the good of his people. Lead faithfully in this way, and your people will follow.

Lift Up the Example of Others Publicly

A model to care for widows doesn't solely have to come from a pastor or deacon. Seize key opportunities to praise and lift up laypeople in your church who faithfully care for widows. For example, take the opportunity during members' meetings to highlight a faithful deacon or young mother who sacrificially cared for a widow that week, and give thanks for their efforts and faithfulness. As you lift up those who are faithful to visit and care for widows, God often will use that example as a way to inspire others to do the same.

This book is intended to aid pastors in the faithful shepherding of their flocks—widows in particular. Yet it is also to be used to teach a flock to care for each other and equip the church of Jesus Christ to minister grace to these hurting ladies within the flock. May God use the platform he has given pastors to urge others to obey God's Word in the care of widows so that these precious saints might experience God's care through the hands and feet of the body of Christ.

13

Stay a While

Silence and solitude for most of us is a needed spiritual discipline in the Christian life. When we can find it in the midst of our busy lives, it is often considered a welcome gift. Typically it does not last long enough. Silence for widows is different. Silence is not a temporary refuge from the craziness of life, but it is where they live most of the time. Silence is usually a snare for the widow, not a gift to embrace. This silence daily reminds them of what they have lost and magnifies the loneliness they feel. Because of this, one of the best practical ways to care for widows is to go where they are, visit with them, and stay a while. One of the most important questions to ask as you consider visiting a widow is how long to stay. How long is "a while" exactly?

"A while" is long enough to make her feel she has had quality time with you. It is long enough to make her feel she was worth your visit. It is long enough to distract her from the eerie silence she experiences most of the time. And yet, how long is truly long enough? The three most common scenarios where you'd visit a widow will be a hospital, her own home, or a nursing home. Because of the unique circumstances surrounding each location, there will be a different amount of time required to "stay a while" yet not stay too long.

Hospital

A helpful starting place when it comes to hospital visitation for widows is to consider the wise words of Alistair Begg:

> It is always better that people should feel our visit is too short than too long.[10]

With this in mind, most recommend no longer than five to ten minutes in a hospital. If widows are in the hospital, it is a safe assumption that they are in some level of pain or quite possibly at the end of their lives. Because of this, we care for them more faithfully by not staying too long. How soon should we visit once we have received word of their illness? This depends upon the condition and affliction of the person. In the nineteenth century people died of ordinary illnesses. This explains why David Dickson writes:

> When the elder does hear of such illness, he should visit *at once*. A day's, or even an hour's, unnecessary delay may cause him a long regret.[11]

In the age of modern medicine, there may not be the sense of urgency there was a hundred or two hundred years ago. There are emergencies, however, that should become our top priority once we receive word of them. Like Dickson, if we tarry and miss the passing of a dear widow in Christ because of our procrastination, we too will experience unnecessary regret. So then, when visiting widows in the hospital, it is wise to prioritize the visit and not stay too long.

Home

A visit to a widow's home needs to be viewed quite differently from a visit to a hospital. In a hospital, her physical condition needs to be most on our radar, and how we conduct ourselves needs to be driven by that reality. A visit to a widow's home shifts the focus. This does not mean there are not physical issues a widow may be battling, but if she is still able to live in her home by herself, this usually means she is healthy enough to care responsibly for herself. The shift in our focus now needs to be directed to her and her home.

Never make a widow feel she must host you when visiting her in a hospital, but when you visit her in her home, allow her to serve you if she offers. When you go to a widow's home, the thing that might bring her the most joy is not just having someone in her home to visit her but having someone to serve. Staying a while may mean staying long enough for a widow to make you coffee or even a meal. It may mean getting the full tour of her home as she talks you through every picture on the wall and every home renovation she and her husband did in the course of the last fifty years. It is not uncommon to stay forty-five to fifty minutes in a widow's home to make her feel as if she has been cared for well and the distraction from the silence is felt.

Nursing Home

A nursing home can be viewed as a middle category between hospital and home and can serve a widow in a couple of different scenarios. It can be that place where widows go to die. Alternatively, though weakness or sickness is present, death might not be imminent, and they just need a place for more extended care. Another use of a nursing home, which is the more common one, is to have a place where widows can go when they no longer can fully care for themselves in their own homes. Oftentimes, one spouse takes care of the other as old age approaches. Once that caregiving spouse is gone, it leaves the other spouse trying to do what he or she so desperately wants to do but can no longer do—care for themselves alone. A nursing home provides that twenty-four-hour care for someone, yet it tries to empower a person to live as independently within that facility as is safe and responsible.

This "home away from home" setup that nursing homes provide creates particular challenges for the visitor to find that balance that makes a widow feel cared for. If someone is in a nursing home because they are close to death, then the hospital principle cited earlier would apply to your visit. If a nursing home is creating a more controlled living space for a relatively healthy but frail widow, however, then it should be treated more like a cautious home visit. Since you want to be more sensitive to the struggles of loneliness than the discomfort of physical pain and suffering, visitors should feel a freedom to stay a bit longer—twenty to thirty minutes. Since the nursing home is commonly viewed as the transition point between hospital and home, it is good to be considerate of both taking an interest in her living space as well as any health concerns that may be present.

• • •

There are other places where you may find yourself visiting a widow, but these are the three most common scenarios that create a template to think through other living situations. Regardless of the location, the spiritual, emotional, and physical condition of the widow is most important. The condition of the widow should dictate how long to stay and how long not to stay. It should determine what will make this widow feel loved and cared for or what might exasperate her. As God gives you wisdom in these case-by-case moments, know that God can use you, even for a moment, to remove the eerie silence and minister grace to these precious ladies.

14

Listen and Learn

It was no secret. Everyone knew. Mrs. Tillie Roberts was one of my favorite widows to visit. Tillie Roberts lived to be 106 years old, just three months shy of her next birthday. Even up to her final days, she had a mind like a steel trap. She drove herself to church until she was 103 years old. She had been widowed some forty years ago, never remarried, and continued to live in her home by herself. She would run into my wife and four children at the grocery store and could even remember their names and birthdays! She loved Jesus. She loved our church. She was always kind and supportive of me as her pastor. She was an amazing lady.

In the midst of my visits with her throughout the years, Tillie taught me a lot of things. One of the most important lessons that has benefited me as a pastor and has proven valuable specifically in the care of widows is the discipline to listen and learn. This was not hard with Tillie. Not only am I a history buff, but this woman had lived almost four times the life I had! Only a fool would not want to listen and learn from this seasoned woman. The question is: What should we listen for and hope to learn?

Listen

When caring for a widow, especially when sitting with her in her home, first listen to her story about her life. Allow her to tell you about her life growing up and her life with her husband—and listen. Listen as she shares about how they met and how she knew she was to marry her husband. Allow her to share about their early years of marriage and the financial challenges they faced at different points in their life together—and listen. Listen in regard to their children and grandchildren, if they were blessed to have them. Listen to the way they made a living and the different places where they lived. Allow her to share about her home, give the tour, and immerse you in her world that the décor in her home represents—and listen.

Second, listen to her spiritual journey with Christ. Listen to her testimony of how she came to see her need for Jesus—listen and rejoice. Allow her to share about her church growing up and her history with her church that you pastor—and listen. Listen as she shares what passages from God's Word are most meaningful to her. Inquire about those who may have discipled her and why those relationships were so meaningful. Hear about her sufferings and how her faith sustained her through them—listen carefully. Have questions to ask and just listen. Follow up with additional questions if needed and just listen. Listening allows her to feel the value of her life and all the Lord has done in it. It provides a healthy avenue to continue the grieving process. It also provides a chance for you to learn.

Learn

What do we uniquely learn as we listen to widows? There are just a few occasions in life when a person speaks with a clarity and perspective that comes only after experiencing deep loss. The loss of a spouse is certainly one of those moments. As you ask questions and listen, you will first of all learn about this precious saint entrusted to your care. You will learn about her life, her joys and struggles, the sufferings she has endured, her painful losses, and exciting victories. You will learn about her faith, how Christ saved her, things about the church you pastor that you may not know, how Christ walked with her through sufferings, and how Christ has ministered grace to her throughout her life.

No doubt if you ask the right questions and listen well, you will not only learn about her and about her life, but you will also learn about your own. Because of the sufferings widows have endured and the daily suffering they face, their strong faith in Jesus Christ and trust in the sovereign goodness of God is uniquely powerful. It is tragic the way so many in the church today view elderly members as a burden weighing down the congregation from moving forward. Yet elderly widows are some of the most insightful members to listen to and learn from because of all they have endured with a steadfast faith throughout the decades.

I learned so much from Tillie Roberts as I listened. I visited her in her home where she shared with me pictures, special furniture, places she had fallen, and her enduring faith in Jesus. I used to ask her to tell me stories of her childhood, the Great Depression, and what life was like without cars, planes, television, or the Internet. She is the only person I knew who could explain all the different ancient farming tools that hung on the walls of Cracker Barrel.[12] I listened and learned from her. When I conducted her funeral, I remembered all I had learned about history from her that gave me a helpful perspective; all I had learned about her life that equipped me to care for her better; all I had learned about our church that made me a more wise pastor; and, all I had learned about her enduring faith that challenged me to strive for the same faithfulness. These are the special moments that await all who would seek to care for these special and unique ladies, but the time must be given to them. When you are with them—listen and learn.

15

Write a Card

The early years of my ministry at my local church were quite difficult. As hostility grew in different camps, other people would naturally get pulled into them. It was a hard and lonely time. And yet there were a few folks who remained steadfast in support and encouraged me in my efforts. There were those who could look past the dysfunctions of the church and the young, rookie mistakes that I was making and still see the Lord was at work.

There was one lady in particular who modeled this foresight. She was an elderly widow. She came early and always made the coffee before Sunday school. She always had a smile on her face and looked for ways to encourage others. She had a special way of encouraging me during those dark and difficult early years. About once a month, she would write me a card and slide it under the door to my office. She would time it so that I would find it on Sunday morning, usually after having to deal with some difficult conflict as I entered the church building. Her cards always contained the same message, yet they freshly lifted my soul every time:

> Pastor, I have been praying for this church for over twenty years and you are the answer to my prayers. You are being faithful. Keep pressing on. Keep preaching the Word. Know that I am praying for you and am with you.

It is hard to express in words what the Lord's grace meant to me in those moments. What I can express to you is how meaningful it was to receive those providentially timed notes of encouragement from this amazing woman. This very easy practical lesson that I learned from this precious widow caused me to see how powerfully God can use a simple note written in the right way at the right time. The two most appropriate times and places to write a card for a widow are when she is in the hospital or experiencing a particularly lonely time.

Notes at the Hospital, Nursing Home, or Rehab Facility

When I first started hospital visitations, I often found my efforts and time were in vain. This was not because of a bad visit but because I would not get to see the sick. So I would leave and try to come back a few hours later but would miss them again. I found myself wasting valuable time driving back and forth, with my efforts continually being met with discouragement. Unfortunately, no one had told me this simple and obvious tactic—leave a note.

There are numerous situations in which widows you have gone to visit will be unavailable. In hospitals, they may have been taken for a test on another floor. They may be unconscious. They may be with a doctor or nurse and not taking visitors. In nursing homes, they may be in an activity or sleeping. In rehab centers, they leave their room to do therapy several times a day. Leaving a note in these kinds of scenarios has been a very helpful and fruitful solution. Leaving a note communicates and accomplishes several aspects of care that you would have pursued had you been able to see them. Here is an example of the kind of simple handwritten note I usually leave:

> Dear _____,
>
> Sorry I [we] missed you. Know that I am praying for you and trusting God's sovereign plans and purposes for you in this difficult time. I talked with the nurse [or family] and will let the congregation know of your updated circumstances. Please let me know if there is any way I can serve you or your family through this time. You can reach me day or night at this number: ________.
>
> Grateful for you,
> Brian and [any others with you]

A note lets a widow know that we took the time to

come, we are praying for her, we want to serve her any way we can, and that she is still connected to the local church despite her circumstances. She can read this note over and over again for encouragement long after you have gone.

Notes Sent to the Widow's Home

It is always good to send an encouraging card to a widow in her home. There are, however, certain key times that an encouraging card to anyone who has lost a spouse would be particularly meaningful. The first and most obvious is on the anniversary of the death of a widow's husband. To us, it is just another day. For a woman who has lost her husband, this is the day she most likely relives the pain and loss, regardless of how long ago it was. Sending a card to a widow on a day like this can prove to be immeasurably helpful and comforting. The content of this card will need to be written a bit differently than one delivered to the hospital:

> Dear __________,
>
> I am writing to let you know I am thinking of you on what may be this most difficult of days. I assume no amount of years makes the pain that this day represents go away. We are praying for you that our sympathetic High Priest, Jesus Christ, would prove to be near for you to call upon him so you might find rest for your weary soul today. Know that we love you and appreciate you in so many ways and are here for you in whatever you need. Please call on us if we can be of

any service to you. But, we are also praying the Holy Spirit might minister to you in a unique and special way today that will counter the deep loneliness that is most certain to come as you reflect on your loss. You can reach me at this number if we can be of service to you: __________.

Grateful for you,
Brian and family

A widow tempted to relive the loss and dwell in the pain has something else to focus on with this note. She can know she is loved, appreciated, and prayed for by those who are asking Jesus to minister to her lonely soul. Instead of just dwelling on what she has lost, she is also reminded of what she still has. Because it is in the form of a card, she can read it over and over again and be reminded of this reality in the days to come.

The elderly widow who ministered to me so significantly in my early years of ministry began to have failing health. She was no longer able to make it to church. She could no longer make the coffee for everyone. Instead, for her final few years, she found herself in and out of hospitals, rehab centers, and eventually a nursing home. Thankfully, I had learned from her example the best way to minister to her soul and encourage her in failing health. I wrote her notes and left them for her in the hospital. I sent cards to her home. I encouraged the rest of the church to write cards and send them to her during the key moments of loneliness she was experiencing.

Toward the end of her life, I went to see her while she was in a nursing home. I walked in and looked on the wall to see a giant bulletin board. It was full of handwritten notes that had been sent to her. I saw notes I had written her years before, and I saw cards that church members had sent that month. That bulletin board may have been her most prized possession as she told me how the Lord had upheld her in difficult days because of the prayers and encouragements of God's people represented on that wall.

Writing a card and sending it to a widow may sound like a very small, simple, even trite way to reach out to someone who is hurting. But for those who have received a card in a significant moment of loneliness and hurt, it can be one of the most powerful ways to minister to anyone—especially a lonely widow.

16

Take a Gift

Everyone loves to receive gifts. Some appreciate them more than others, but most people—whether they feel particularly loved by gifts or not—appreciate the sentiment of the gift from the giver. A gift says, "I love and appreciate you," grounded in the thoughtfulness and intentionality of the whole process. In the same way, giving a gift to a widow can be a particularly encouraging gesture. Widows were wives, and many of them are mothers and grandmothers. It is safe to say that many of them made sacrificial efforts to give gifts to the ones to whom they sought to communicate the most love. They know the level of thoughtfulness and effort required to give a gift that is meaningful to a particular person. A widow, just like other specific people in your life, is uniquely encouraged by gifts that speak to a certain need she may have. For the widow, a needed gift, a consumable gift, or a sentimental gift are some of the most significant gifts she can receive that often uniquely minister to her. Additionally deacons in the local church can lead in the gathering and distribution of these gifts to meet these needs, similar to the men set apart in the early church to meet the physical needs of widows (Acts 6:1–7).

A Needed Gift

Have you ever heard someone say, "I need that newest iPhone," or, "I need that movie as soon as it comes out on Blu-ray." Some have actually convinced themselves these are things they truly needed. Obviously, those are wants camouflaged as needs and are not the gifts to which I am referring. A needed gift is something that would help meet a basic requirement that a widow has in order to live out her daily life. For example, we have an international refugee who is a widow with several children in our congregation. She is not concerned with the latest iPhone but with what her children will eat for that day. She is not concerned with what movies are being released but with whether or not she will be evicted from her apartment. These kinds of widows have many needs that a pastor can lead his church to help provide. Whether it is food, toiletries, money, or clothes, a gift that meets an immediate need for a widow is a very biblical way to serve her and can act as a great encouragement to her as she sees God's provision come through his church.

The colder weather of winter poses greater challenges for the elderly widows. These greater needs come in two forms. The first is increased outdoor upkeep on their property that most elderly widows are physically unable to do. The second is the long, dark, cold nights that can heighten the tendency to depression and prolong feelings of loneliness. Here are some practical ways to provide for the physical needs of widows, particularly as the weather gets cold:

- rake leaves;
- clean gutters;
- shovel snow from the driveways;
- provide rides to and from church or the doctor;
- change light bulbs; or
- just go and fix something in their home.

These are all wonderful ways to meet the physical needs of elderly widows. Those who can pull this off without them knowing it give a particularly sweet gift.

An Edible Gift

On the other side of this coin, there are some widows who have lived a long time and have no financial or physical needs. A husband was wise with his money before he died and made sure his wife would be taken care of. Additionally, there are some elderly widows' homes that have so many knickknacks that the last thing you want to bring is another one to crowd the shelf. Instead, make something that she can eat or drink. Do some research and find out what goodies she used to make and take to all the shut-ins in the church before she was unable to get out anymore. Find out what her favorite coffee or tea is and wrap it up with a nice bow and personally deliver it to her. One Christmas, my wife made special chocolates with my young children, and they all went to deliver some to each of the elderly widows in our congregation. Just because a widow may not have immediate daily physical needs doesn't mean there are no other ways to brighten her day and remind her she is not forgotten.

A Sentimental Gift

The most meaningful gifts I receive are not the most expensive or the latest gadget but the ones that are made just for me. In my family, the most meaningful gifts I receive are the cards my young children make me or the thoughtful handwritten cards from my wife. The gifts that truly communicate thoughtfulness are the most meaningful. Widows are no different. In fact, I would say this is even more true for the widow who desires to be known, heard, and acknowledged more than having any trinket to go on the shelf. One of the best ways to give a gift like this is to find out what kinds of sweet, sentimental gifts a widow's husband used to give her, and then give something similar. In some contexts, this might be more appropriate to receive from another lady in the church or the pastor's wife. These gifts are the ones that can often lift the spirits of a grieving widow, as they not only communicate a thoughtfulness commonly absent in her life but they remind her of the way her husband used to love her and they give her a brief moment to feel that love once more.

Ministering grace to a widow with a gift is not just about the gift but the message communicated to the widow by the gift. Do the work to find out what physical needs are there, bake some goodies like she used to bake, or simply have your children make a card that says you appreciate her. It is in those moments when a gift is used by God in ways you cannot know or anticipate that it acts as a simple reminder to a widow that she is not forgotten.

17

Involve Your Family

One of the most difficult funerals I have ever conducted was the funeral of a young deacon in our church. He was a dear friend who had been killed in a car crash and left a wife and young family behind. As I look back on that very painful time, what sticks out was the essential role my wife played in our efforts to care for this shocked widow who was naturally experiencing deep grief. Pastors call upon their wives for many things within their ministry in the local church, but I realized one of the most significant is ministering to other women who are in crisis. Whether it is a young widow who suddenly loses her husband or a woman who just lost her husband of fifty years, a pastor's family is an invaluable resource to care for these ladies and can act as an example that encourages other families in the church to serve in similar ways. There are many fruitful reasons for a pastor to involve both his wife and children in the care of widows.

Involve Your Wife

As your wife seeks to care for older widows especially, it provides an opportunity for a younger woman to care for an older woman. Elderly widows appreciate care from anyone in the church, but they seem to love care from younger women. I am not sure if it is the feeling of a daughter's care, but my experience shows a clear, meaningful distinction from visits by young women than from any others.

In the midst of your wife's effort, God also provides an opportunity for an older woman to instruct and encourage a younger one (Titus 2:3–4). These interactions potentially provide an opportunity for a young woman to gain wise instruction from an older woman, a young mom to receive counsel from an older mom. We have an elderly widow in her midnineties who was married over fifty years and had seven children (including one set of twins). As you can imagine, this woman is an endless resource of wisdom and insight for young women, wives, and moms. Young women in the church should love to learn from these kinds of ladies. These elderly widows love having their many years of experience used to serve Christ's people.

In regard to younger widows, a pastor's wife can be a very special friend and companion. Additionally, pastors need to be especially mindful to involve their wives in the care of younger widows, not just for the companionship of another woman for that widow, but also to keep you as a pastor from putting yourself into an unwise position with regard to a very vulnerable woman in your congregation. Sadly, I have watched a pastor leave his wife to marry a younger widow in his congregation. A pastor should never underestimate the emotions stirred in these moments and needs to place a particular guard between himself and the hurting widow seeking his care. A pastor's wife can act as a buffer that allows a pastor to minister closely to a young widow but still remain above reproach.

There are also wonderful ways for a wife to minister through her children. Since moms are typically on a set schedule when their kids are little, it provides open times for them to go and visit widows and take their children with them at a time that is convenient. This schedule also provides open slots of availability during the day, which is typically the best time to visit elderly widows. As children become older, they are able to engage and serve widows in their own ways that can become very meaningful to widows and make the children feel they are serving the church in a significant way.

Children bless widows. One of the greatest gifts you can give an elderly widow is to take a child with you to visit her. Most elderly widows love children. Many of them have grown children of their own who maybe live far away, which means visits from their children and grandchildren are infrequent. They love to just watch a child. Talk to them. Play with them. Hear you tell stories about them. Interacting with a child often becomes an elderly widow's most precious and memorable weekly moment. This is a tremendous opportunity for the pastor's wife to use her children at any age or stage of life to minister in a meaningful way.

Involve Your Children

As I buried a certain beloved widow in our church, I was reminded of the fruitful effects that children can have on the lives of the elderly, and likewise, the influence the elderly can have on our children. When I brought my family to the funeral of this widow to say goodbye, something unexpected happened. We were greeted by members of this woman's family that I had never met, but they somehow knew my children and even their names because she had talked to her family about them all the time out of her love for them.

The family was so excited to meet these "famous" children that this widow always talked about. I began to realize my children had helped me care for this woman through the years and bring joy to her life in a way that I could not have done visiting her by myself. She dearly loved children but never had any of her own. She loved mine. It is one of the many reasons I dearly loved and appreciated this woman. There are several benefits for a pastor to include his children in the care of widows and to encourage other parents to do the same.

First, never underestimate the impact of children in the lives of others. Those of us who are parents know that children are a gift from God. Yet, it is important for parents to realize their children are also a gift to others if we are willing to share them. There are elderly widows in our church whose weeks are made so special when a church member goes to visit them with the children.

Second, it is good for a child to learn to love, grieve, and let go. I was reminded of this as we drove away from the visitation and my two oldest daughters (then seven and ten years old) began to cry. Although I do not like to see my daughters cry, it reminded me that this widow's affection for them and my children's affection for her were mutual. Parents mistakenly want to shelter their children from this aspect of life when they are younger. But these moments are wonderful times from God to help our children understand death, be grateful for knowing these special people in our lives, and ultimately see why we so badly need the hope of the gospel.

Lastly, it will cause the young and old to see the value of the other. The multigenerational local church is fading into the past. This should not be. The best way for us to fight against it is to do the things that cause young and old to grow in Christian love and affection for each other. I was so grateful for this particular widow's contribution throughout the years. For in the absence of having her own children, she loved so many in the church as if they were her own.

A pastor's family is so valuable to a pastor and his ministry. It will require a bit more planning and intentionality to include them, but the benefits are well worth it. A pastor will find a special joy not just in including and instructing his family to care for others who are hurting and lonely, but also in allowing them to see the impact it can have on those to whom he ministers—particularly widows.

18

Enjoy Their Company

It can baffle our minds as we seek to care for someone who has lost their soulmate, especially when the person enjoyed that companionship for over fifty years. This is truly a great challenge, but one that God in his grace can equip pastors, deacons, and the rest of the church to do. There is no way to fill the void of a lifelong companion, but there are ways to soften the sting of loneliness that most will always struggle with, regardless of how long ago they lost their spouse. One effective way to care for these dear saints is to find something in their life they enjoyed doing with their spouse, offer to go do it with them, and enjoy their company.

A widower in our church enjoyed sixty-three years of marriage with his wife before he was shocked with her sudden diagnosis of advanced cancer. She died six weeks later. Even years after her death, this man never stopped grieving her loss. There are many ways her death radically changed this man's daily life. One in particular was his pattern of eating meals. He loved going to a restaurant with his wife, but after she died, he stopped going out to eat. Though his love for eating out still remained, he didn't want to sit and eat alone, knowing he would be thinking of his wife and missing her the whole time.

Once I realized through a conversation with him that this was the reason he no longer went to restaurants, I asked if he would be willing to go to a restaurant and eat with me. He was surprised by the offer but took me up on it. We began going to lunch about once every month for the next several years. He beamed every time we went. He loved the company, loved to introduce me to his friends, and loved to tell me the same stories over and over again. Although I invited him out originally, he never let me pay. These outings have provided an opportunity to shepherd and care for him spiritually. I received regular encouragement from him about how meaningful this time had become for him.

As a result of this fruitful experience, several other church members pursued lunch with this man, and the spiritual care he has received from the congregation through this medium has been immeasurable! These times of fellowship and care continued until the day he died, eight years after his wife preceded him in death.

Some of the best ways to care for widows and widowers is to simply spend time with them doing the things they enjoy doing. Ask about their deceased spouse and the things they did together that meant so much. Then, offer to do those things with them. Minister the Word of God to them as you find appropriate opportunities. You will gain insight into those things they loved to do, as well as provide a healthy way for them to continue to grieve their loss. Make the time. Think creatively. You can have confidence you will be as blessed as they are by your efforts. And you will enjoy their company.

19

Watch for Anniversaries

My wedding anniversary is one of the most special days of the year. Each anniversary, I am reminded of the day I joined together with my bride, and we celebrate all the life we have lived together since our wedding. My wife and I have very specific, meaningful activities and discussions on every anniversary. We do this to provide a way to evaluate our marriage and celebrate what the Lord has done the previous year, as well as to identify ways to be more faithful to each other in the future. Most Christian married couples have a similar pattern for their wedding anniversary, but what happens when a spouse dies? As mentioned earlier, this day that once represented one of the happiest days of someone's life now becomes arguably the most painful.

A widow is a unique lady who, now that her husband is gone, not only has this once very special day transformed into a very painful day, but she has also added another anniversary to her annual calendar—the anniversary of her husband's death. Both become very painful days, days that pastors and the church need to be aware are coming in the lives of the widows in their care.

Widowed Anniversary

This day becomes the day every wife dreads to have in her life, that is, the yearly reminder of when her husband passed away. This day brings back the memories all over again of not just the passing of her spouse, but the circumstances surrounding it. It could have been the final day in a long, hard, painful death from cancer or some other horrific disease or illness that finally won. It could also have been the day when that unthinkable phone call came from the police saying that her husband was just killed in a car crash, and it is therefore a day that brings back the memories of having to identify the body and tell her children, "Daddy isn't coming home."

The first widowed anniversary is invariably the most painful and difficult for the widow to cope with. Some widows will prefer to be left alone on that day, while others may thrive on having company. Make sure you discern each individual situation, as it will be different for every widow.

The best way to care for a widow on this day is simply to be aware when this day is approaching and make intentional plans to extend care on that day. If you are writing a card, get it in the mail a couple of days ahead of time so it arrives on the day. If you are able to pay a visit, warm Christian fellowship is a wonderful way to pass the time and help her get through this day. Even a phone call, text, or e-mail can be a meaningful effort on that particular day. No one can take away the painful memories of this day, but what we can do is remind widows that they are loved and not forgotten as the memories of this dreadful day come flooding back.

Wedding Anniversary

We can be certain that every widow, regardless of the duration of her marriage, remembers her wedding anniversary. It becomes, arguably, the hardest day of the year for her. This means that the church should be keenly aware of this day also and seize the opportunity to care for a widow on it. How can we extend care on this day? Find a meaningful way to celebrate this day based on how she used to celebrate it with her husband.

We had an elderly lady in our church lose her husband of over sixty years. A young man in the church recalled her telling the story of what her husband always did for her on their anniversary. Each year, her husband presented her a yellow rose accompanied by a card with handwritten, encouraging words inside.

On the afternoon of her anniversary, this young man arrived at this widow's door with a yellow rose and a handwritten card to give to her. Did this act replace the absent effort of her late husband? Certainly not. The gesture was incredibly meaningful for this woman, however, and it forever changed the relationship she had with this young man. She still talks about how much his gesture meant to her; how thoughtful it was; how much it reminded her of her husband's love for her. That young man now possesses a door into her life to care for her physically and spiritually in ways few others in the church have.

(Do note that while American culture allows for this kind of interaction, some widows in other cultures may see this sort of action as intrusive, not an endeavor to love. Be aware of your place and culture. The point is to find meaningful ways to celebrate the memory of a widow's husband that fits your particular culture and reaches the heart of that grieving widow.)

Ask the widows about their anniversaries. Most will eagerly tell you. Then, do your best to do something meaningful on that day. Remind them on these particularly hard days that they are loved and their pain is not forgotten. Resolve to try and bear this burden with them in any way you can (Gal. 6:2). One thing you can count on: any effort on those particular days—a widow's wedding and widowed anniversaries—will mean more than you can imagine and will ultimately remind her that the Lord is near and knows her grief.

20

Adopt during Holidays

The holidays can be a time of joy for some and sadness for others. A group in the church that almost always experiences sorrow during this time of year is widows. Christmas, Thanksgiving, even birthdays all act as reminders to a widow of her husband's absence, and her family gets preoccupied with other things. Because of the busyness of these celebrations with travel and planning, these are occasions when widows are often forgotten. Pastors, deacons, and the local church can serve widows in meaningful ways, particularly on these annual holidays, by adopting them for a time. In other words, you bring them into your holiday plans as one of your family.

Honor Widows at Church

One of the best ways to honor widows in your church is to have a special dinner at church in their honor at the times when they are usually most neglected—holidays. I once received word of a pastor and his wife who planned a large dinner at the church just to honor the widows and widowers of the church at Christmas. As many of these folks don't have a lot of family around, this is a great time to remind them that the body of Christ is their family. My understanding is that, in addition to eating together, there were special things done and said that made these widows and widowers feel loved, valued, and honored. Widows can also be honored as a focus of our prayer time during the holidays in the public gatherings, bringing encouragement to them and awareness to the congregation that is tempted to forget these ladies in the midst of the holiday scrambling.

Sing to Widows in Their Homes

One of the most fun activities we do as a church is to caravan around to different elderly widows' homes on a Saturday evening close to Christmas and sing Christ-honoring Christmas songs. Everybody brings their children, we have a good time of fellowship, but most importantly, those we sing for and serve through this effort are encouraged and lifted in ways few other efforts seem to accomplish. They are warmed by the fellowship and are reminded that Christ has not forgotten them, nor have Christ's people.

Invite Widows to Your Home

Inviting widows to Thanksgiving or Christmas dinner with your family is a powerful way to adopt a widow into your family. As I look back through the years as a child, some of the Thanksgiving and Christmas dinners that stick out are when we had an elderly widow whom my father had brought to the house at the last minute suddenly join us for dinner. I'm sure the effect on me paled in comparison to the way that dear, sweet, elderly, lonely woman felt when she was able to eat with and be included in our family, instead of sitting at home alone.

Never underestimate the impact you can have by making these efforts with widows and widowers, especially through the holidays. If you step out of your comfort zone to be faithful in these ways, I trust you will not regret the sweet fellowship that you will experience with these dear saints. A merciful God has adopted each one of us who are in Christ into his eternal family through the precious blood of Jesus. Here is a wonderful opportunity to mirror that grace and eternal adoption in the care of a sweet saint who is alone for the holidays.

Conclusion

The evidence is overwhelming, whether we consider the Law and the Prophets in the Old Testament Scriptures or the Lord Jesus Christ and the New Testament church. By precepts, by principles, by warnings, and by example both human and divine, the Scriptures provide the church of Christ with a clear mandate to minister to widows. Job was a man who, despite accusations to the contrary, had cared for the poor, the fatherless, and the widow. He "caused the widow's heart to sing for joy" (Job 29:13). That should be the aim of the church in ministering the grace of God in the Lord Jesus Christ to widows. It is not the only ministry the church should undertake, but it is an integral part of that biblical religion which James defined as "pure and undefiled . . . before God and the Father" (James 1:27).

One Widow's Woe and Joy: A True Story

In postwar South Wales in the 1950s there was a young widow with two children aged nine and five. Her husband had been tragically killed in a motorcycle accident in their mining and farming community some twelve years after they had married. She was plunged into poverty and distress and subsequently suffered two mental breakdowns. Her heart turned against the church in her village because of the hypocrisy that she observed and also because of the attitude exhibited toward her. Unable to afford the pew rent, or the "right" clothes in order to attend church services, she became embittered in her heart. She also knew the men who sat in the "big seat" beneath the pulpit who ran the church, some of whom were deacons. Among them were local businessmen who were regarded as pillars in the community. Despite knowing her tragic circumstances, no help was forthcoming, either financial or practical. She was largely left to fend for herself. The church she attended had lost the gospel and the wonder of God's mercy and grace. This loss was tragically reflected in their attitude toward her as a needy widow. Their religion proved false. They appeared to be devoid of that pure and undefiled religion which is acceptable to God.

Mrs. Gwyneth Jones continued to struggle to make ends meet and provide for her two children. Her daughter became a Christian in her teens, but her mother remained deeply skeptical despite her daughter's best efforts to explain the gospel to her. Soured by her experience, she had no time for the church. She had concluded that it was full of hypocrites. Her children eventually moved away from home, and Gwyneth moved into a council housing estate, not far from her brother and sister-in-law and other relatives.

In due course, with advancing age she moved to southeast England to be near her daughter and family. An ancient London livery company—the Worshipful Company of Dyers—had a charitable foundation that provided sheltered housing for "poor people of good character, able to look after themselves." She came to regard her new home as "her palace." This company, while not openly Christian, showed more compassion to her than the church of her youth.

Her daughter, Mai, married me (Austin) in 1970. We settled in Crawley in 1972, where I subsequently became a pastor of a Baptist church in the town. On Gwyneth's arrival in the late 1970s, I began to visit her on a regular basis and won her confidence sufficiently to obtain her permission to read and explain the Bible and the way of salvation to her. It was a long process and she almost died of cancer before she came to Christ. She lived another five years after recovering from the cancer, but during that time she professed her faith in Christ and told me, "I should have done this years ago." Her woes had finally been turned to joy before she fell asleep in Jesus in 1991, aged 75.

Visiting her regularly, providing practical help where needed, and learning to minister God's grace to her primarily as an unbelieving widow was an invaluable experience for me as a young pastor. My wife of course was heavily involved, as were our children, one of whom became a nurse partly as a result of the experience she gained in visiting and caring for her grandmother.

The Task of the Church

Subsequently, I was called on to show others who became widows in our congregation what the Scriptures taught about God's care for the widow. They were in need of comfort, and that meant opening up some key passages in both the Old and New Testaments. At the same time, when I received an e-mail asking a number of pastors if anyone knew of any books on the subject of ministering to widows, I realized there was little or nothing available. So I simply took my Bible and a concordance and worked my way through every biblical reference to widows and began to share my findings with the widows concerned. At the request of a number of people I put what I had been teaching these widows into a more permanent form.[13]

My study of the Scriptures convinced me that the care of widows should therefore be prominent in the agenda and in the life of every true church of Christ. Elders and deacons, as well as every church member, should be conscious of the biblical rationale and duty to minister to the widows in their company. Pastoral visitation, public prayers, and the financial expenditure of the church ought to reflect this biblical obligation.

Care should be taken to ensure that such a ministry is not motivated merely by humanitarian considerations.

Anyone sensitive to human needs might feel obligated to provide help and relief for a widow. The church of Jesus Christ, however, must be motivated by the grace and compassion of the triune God. A constant awareness of the mercy that we have received lies at the foundation of the church's ministry. If we lose the gospel and the motivation that comes from the gospel, then the ministry we are called to undertake in Christ's name will also be lost. God is rich in mercy and has loved us with a great love (Eph. 2:4–6). The church is to demonstrate that mercy and that love. One of the ways in which she is to do that is by showing care and compassion for the widow and to cause her heart to "sing for joy" (Job 29:13).

Appendix A

The Situation of Widows and Orphans of Christian Ministers

Andrew Fuller

Northamptonshire Baptist Association Circular Letter, 1815, by Andrew Fuller, "The Situation of the Widows and Orphans of Christian Ministers, etc."[14]

Dear brethren, the subject to which we this year invite your attention, is the situation of the widows and orphans of Christian ministers, and of ministers themselves who by age, or permanent affliction, are laid aside from their work.

We have not been used to address you on subjects relating to our own temporal interests; nor is this the case at present; for the far greater part of those who have been most active in forming the institution for which we plead have no expectation of deriving any advantage from it, but, feeling for many of their brethren, they are desirous of alleviating their condition.

Mercy is a distinguishing character of the religion of the Bible, especially to the fatherless and the widow. The great God claims to be their Protector and Avenger. "A Father of the fatherless, and a judge of the widows, is God in his holy habitation"—"Ye shall not afflict any widow, or fatherless child. If thou afflict them in any wise, and they cry at all unto me, I will surely hear their cry; and my wrath shall wax hot, and I will kill you with the sword; and your wives shall be widows, and your children fatherless."[15] Mercy to the fatherless and the widow is introduced as a test of true religion. "Pure religion and undefiled before God and the Father is this, To visit the fatherless and widows in their affliction, and to keep himself unspotted from the world."[16] The affliction of the fatherless and the widow is a subject taken for granted. From the day of their bereavement, dejection takes possession of their dwelling, and imprints its image on every object around them. And when to this is added, that from time to time their sources of the necessaries of life are in a great measure dried up, a full cup of affliction must needs be their portion. At first many feel for them, and weep with them: but time and a number of similar cases wear away these impressions; and, being unprotected, it is well if they be not exposed to oppression; and even where there is no particular want of kindness towards them, yet their cases, being but little known, are often but little regarded.

The widow and fatherless children of ministers have peculiar claims on the benevolence of the churches. The ministerial profession, like that of arms, requires the subjects of it, if possible, not to "entangleth himself with the affairs of this life; that he may please him who hath chosen him to be a soldier."[17] On this ground, a large proportion of ministers, living entirely on the contributions of their hearers, have no opportunity of providing for their families after their decease. You, brethren, by the blessing of God on your diligent attention to business, are generally enabled to meet this difficulty. You have business in which to bring up your children from their early years; but they seldom have: and when you have taught them an honourable calling, you can spare something to set them up in trade; but it is rarely so with them.

Yet the post occupied by your ministers is honourable and important. Regardless of the sneers of the irreligious, they feel it to be so. To be chosen and approved by a Christian congregation, next to the choice and approbation of Christ, is their highest ambition. This honour, however, involves them in circumstances which require your consideration. You expect them to maintain a respectable appearance, both in their persons and families; but to do this, and at the same time to pay every one his due, often renders it impossible to provide for futurity.

Our churches, when in want of ministers, are solicitous to obtain men of talent. There may be an excess in this desire, especially where personal godliness is overlooked; and it is certain that great talents are far from being common. But view Christian ministers as a body, and we may appeal to you whether they be not possessed of talents, which, if employed in business, would with the blessing of God, ordinarily bestowed on honest industry, have rendered both them and their families equally comfortable with you and yours. And shall their having relinquished these temporal advantages to serve the cause of Christ, and to promote your spiritual welfare, be at the expense of the comfort of their widows and children when they have finished their course?

In the persecuting times which preceded the revolution of 1688, our Protestant Dissenting forefathers had but little encouragement to provide for futurity, as the fruits of their industry were taken from them: but it is not so with us; our property is secure; and we are therefore able to contribute to those benevolent objects which tend to the good of mankind.

It was an object that attracted the attention of our fathers, early in the last century, to provide for the widows of their ministers; and a noble fund it is which was then established in London for the widows of the three denominations. Besides this, a liberal plan has been pursued within the last two-and-twenty years to increase the sum, by an addition from the profits of a magazine. It is not to supersede these benevolent means of relief, but to add to them according to the exigencies of the times, and to include not only widows, but superannuated ministers and orphans, that societies like ours have of late been formed in various counties and religious connexions.

The case of superannuated ministers, or ministers who by affliction are permanently laid aside from their work, has a serious influence on the well-being of the churches. Where no provision of this kind is made, every humane and Christian feeling revolts at the idea of dismissing an aged and honourable man, even though his work is done. Yet if the congregation continue to support him, they may be unable to support another. The consequence is, in a few years the congregation has dwindled almost to nothing. To meet these cases, along with those of the fatherless and the widow, is the object of this institution.

Brethren, we feel it an honour to be supported by the free contributions of those whom we serve in the gospel of Christ. To receive our support as an expression of love renders it doubly valuable. And if you view things in a right light, you will esteem it a privilege on your part. If your places of worship were ready built for you, your ministers supported, and their families provided for, would it be better? Would you feel equally interested in them? Would you not feel as David did when Araunah the Jebusite offered his thrashing-floor, his oxen, and his wood? "Nay . . . neither will I offer burnt offerings unto the LORD my God of that which doth cost me nothing!"[18]

Should any object that ministers ought to set an example of trust in their heavenly Father, who knoweth what things they need, and of leaving their widows and fatherless children with him; we answer, when all is done that can be done to alleviate their wants, there will be abundant occasion for these graces. The trust that we are called to place in our heavenly Father does not however preclude the exercise of prudent foresight, either in ourselves, or in the friends of Christ towards us for his sake.

It is one of the most lovely features of our mission in the East [Carey and Serampore], that, while our brethren are disinterestedly giving up all their temporal acquirements to the cause in which they are engaged, they have provided an asylum for their widows and orphans; so that when a missionary dies, he has no painful anxiety what is to become of them. They have a home, which some have preferred to their native country. Is it any distrust of the Lord's goodness to be thus tender of those who are flesh of their flesh and bone of their bone, and who have helped to bear the burden of their cares? Say, rather, is it not a truly Christian conduct? But, if so, why should we not go and do likewise?

It is one of the most endearing traits in the character of our Lord Jesus Christ, that, while the salvation of the world was pending, he did not neglect to provide for his aged mother. Joseph is thought to have been dead for some years, and Mary seems to have followed Jesus, who, while upon earth, discharged every branch of filial duty and affection towards her. But now that he is going to his Father, who shall provide for her? Looking down from the cross on her, and on his beloved disciple, he saith to the one, "Behold thy son!" and to the other, "Behold thy mother!"

What exquisite sensibility do these words convey! To her it was saying, "Consider me as living in my beloved disciple"; and to him, "Consider my mother as your own." It is no wonder that "from that hour that disciple took her unto his own home."[19]

We live in times very eventful; and it cannot have escaped your observation that the success of the gospel has kept pace with the mighty changes which have agitated the world. Never, perhaps, were there such great calls on our liberality as of late years, and never were more honourable exertions made. Yet God, that giveth us all things richly to enjoy, has not suffered us to want, and has promised to supply all our need according to his riches in glory by Christ Jesus.

Appendix B

A Unique Ministry

Training Young Mothers to Care for Elderly Widows

One of the most helpful assets to a pastor in the local church in regard to caring for elderly widows is the stay-at-home mom. Here are five practical ways a pastor can train young moms in his church to take their children and visit elderly widows. Once a list has been created of those widows by the pastors, have the young moms begin to:

1. *Pray and contact.* A great place to start is to take that list of widows that the pastors have put together and have the young mom set a goal to pray and write a handwritten card to each widow on that list in one month. This allows a young mom who may be a bit

apprehensive about visiting to make the first contact and allow God to stir her affections for these widows through praying for them.

2. *Organize a scheduled visit.* Next, the young mom should take the list and systematically begin to work her way down the list, setting a goal to maybe visit one or two widows a week. Once she completes the list it will be time to start the list over again.

3. *Bake or make something to take as a gift.* Widows love to receive any gift that a young mom might bring with her. Whether she bakes cookies, makes something, or has her children color a picture, never underestimate the value of bringing something for widows to look at, eat, or admire for days after the young mom has left.

4. *Make a list of prayer requests.* At some point in the visit, the young mom should pull out a pad and pen and ask, "What are some things you would like the pastors and the whole church body to be praying on your behalf?" This is helpful to the pastors and a wonderful way to communicate a desire to care for the widow's needs.

5. *Write a brief report of the visit for the pastors.* After the young mom leaves, she should write a brief e-mail to one of the pastors by the end of the week of how the visit went and the prayer requests she gathered from the widow. This allows the pastors to pray more specifically for the widow and more accurately inform the congregation of her needs.

Frequently Asked Questions

Lastly, let me address two of the most common questions asked by young moms.

"How Long Should We Stay?"

Anywhere from 15–45 minutes is a good template (barring comfort level, kids' meltdowns, etc.).

"What Should We Talk About?"

Topics such as how the widow is feeling, the family members caring for her, a typical day, history about her life, her testimony of conversion, marriage and child-rearing advice, and ways to pray for her are all great ways to carry a conversation.

• • •

Pastors, be training young moms in your congregation. Young moms are capable of having a very meaningful ministry in this area if you encourage them to step out in faith believing God will give the words and compassion needed to care for these ladies.

Acknowledgments

Austin and Brian would like to thank . . .

Crossway for their enthusiastic investment in this work and Laura Talcott in particular, who edited the original manuscript. Thank you for your partnership and seeing the importance of this book to serve pastors and equip Christ's church in this noble task.

Jeremy Walker for using his invaluable editorial gifts and insightful comments to serve us both. This work will better serve others because of your contribution.

The local congregations we are so blessed to serve—Maidenbower Baptist Church and Auburndale Baptist Church. We count it an unspeakable joy and privilege to shepherd these flocks on behalf of the Chief Shepherd until he returns.

The precious widows in our churches God entrusted to our care throughout the years, some of whom have gone to be with their Lord. Whatever care we provided for you pales in comparison to what we learned from you and how we benefited from knowing you.

Our families, particularly our wives, Mai and Cara. Other than Christ, there is no greater gift either of us has received than you, your love, and your companionship.

Our great God and Savior Jesus Christ, who by his sovereign grace purchased our salvation with his own blood and appointed us as undershepherds of his redeemed people. This is a most undeserved gift and is why all praise and glory go to him alone!

Notes

1. For further details see Richard D. Patterson, "The Widow, Orphan, and the Poor in the Old Testament and Extra-Biblical Literature," *Bibliotheca Sacra*, July 1973: 223–34.
2. Key passages are Isaiah 1:16–18, 23; 10:1–3; Jeremiah 7:7; 15:7–9; 22:2–4; Ezekiel 22:6–18, 24–26; Zechariah 7:9–11; and Malachi 3:5.
3. Key passages are Exodus 22:21–24 and Deuteronomy 24:16–18; 27:19.
4. For a detailed consideration of the redeemer and levirate laws being considered here, see Donald A. Leggett, *The Levirate and Goel Institutions in the Old Testament with Special Attention to the Book of Ruth* (Cherry Hill, NJ: Mack, 1974).
5. Levirate law provides for the marriage of the widow to a brother of the deceased in order to raise up children and maintain the family name. When Boaz marries Ruth, however, he does so not as another son of Elimelech and Naomi. He acts as a *goel*, a redeemer. He marries Ruth and they have a son, Obed, thus preserving the family line.
6. Derek Kidner, *Psalms 73–150: A Commentary on Books III–V of the Psalms* (London: Inter-Varsity, 1975), 402.
7. David L. McKenna, *Mark*, The Communicator's Commentary (Dallas, TX: Word Books, 1982), 257–58.
8. There are different opinions about whether Scripture recognizes a separate order of female deacons or whether the "women" of

1 Timothy 3:11 are deacons' wives. There is no biblical term for "deaconess"; the masculine form of *diakonos* was used for both men and women. Thus, in Romans 16:1, Phoebe is described as a "servant [*diakonos*]" of the church in Cenchreae. Personally, I am not convinced there is a separate order of female deacons. At the same time, I would affirm that there are crucial roles for women to play in the life and ministry of the church and that those roles should be publicly acknowledged.

9. Curtis Thomas, *Practical Wisdom for Pastors: Words of Encouragement and Counsel for a Lifetime of Ministry* (Wheaton, IL: Crossway, 2001), 104.
10. Derek Prime and Alistair Begg, *On Being a Pastor: Understanding Our Calling and Work* (Chicago: Moody, 2004), 175.
11. David Dickson, *The Elder and His Work* (Phillipsburg, NJ: P&R, 2004), 60, italics in original.
12. Cracker Barrel is a restaurant found all throughout the United States. Its décor most resembles the culture of the Southern states, including old farming tools used in the late nineteenth century and other aspects of American history in the South.
13. This material found its way into Austin Walker, *God's Care for the Widow* (Leominster, UK: Day One, 2010).
14. Joseph Belcher, ed., *The Complete Works of Andrew Fuller*, vol. 3 (1845, repr., Penn Laird, VA: Sprinkle, 1988), 363–66.
15. Psalm 68:5; Exodus 22:22–24 KJV.
16. James 1:27 KJV.
17. 2 Timothy 2:4 KJV.
18. 2 Samuel 24:24 KJV.
19. John 19:26–27 KJV.

For more information about
Practical Shepherding, go to:
practicalshepherding.com